WOODEN TOYS

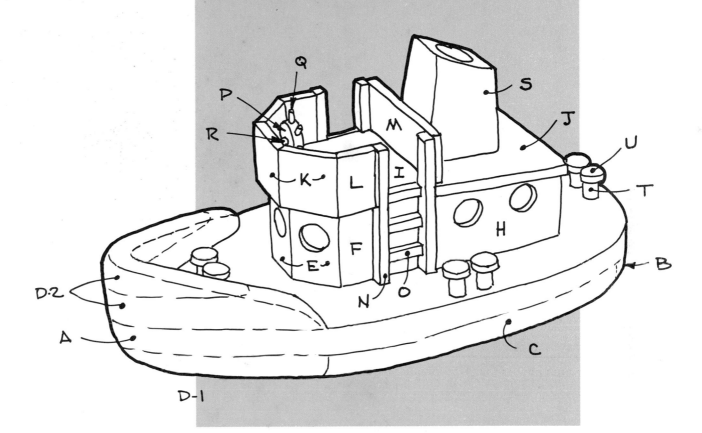

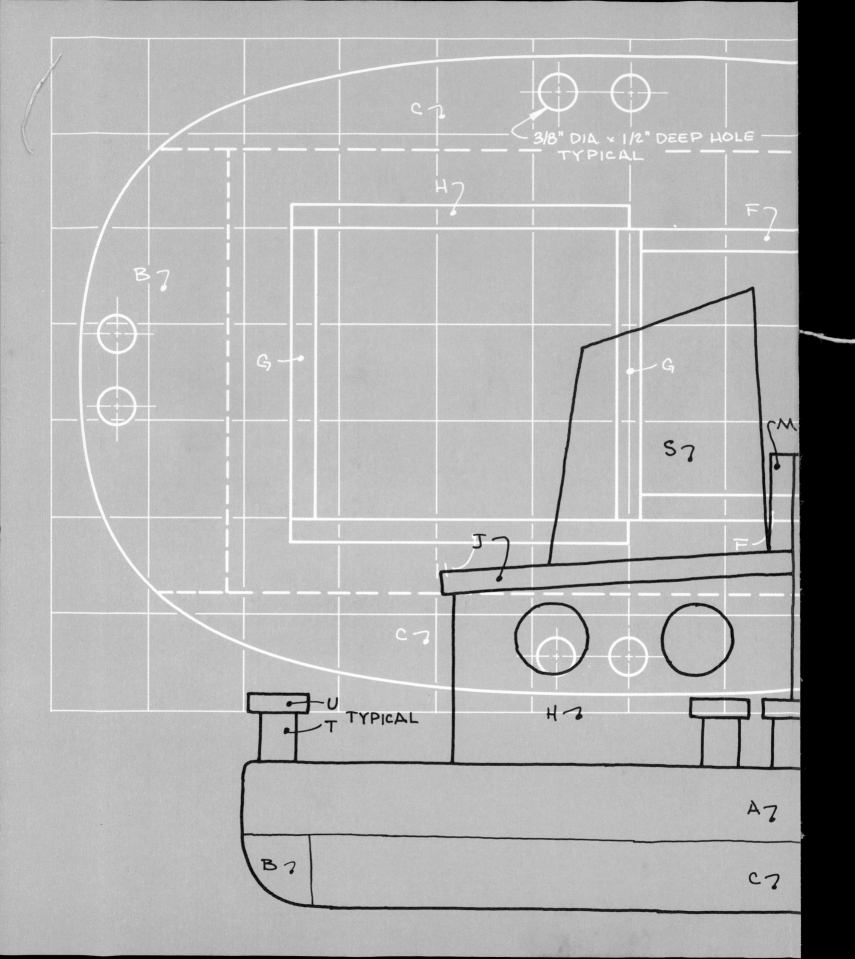

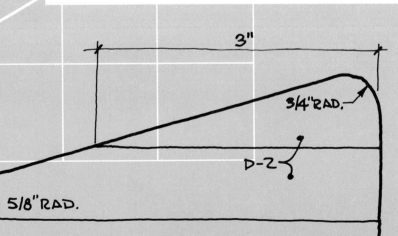

WOODEN TOYS

by GENE and
KATIE HAMILTON

Illustrations by
STEVE WOLGEMUTH

Sedgewood® Press
NEW YORK

For CBS, Inc.:
    Editorial Director: Dina von Zweck
    Project Coordinator: Jacqueline Weinbach

For Sedgewood® Press:
    Director: Elizabeth P. Rice
    Project Editor: Bruce Macomber
    Associate Editor: Leslie Gilbert
    Production Manager: Bill Rose

Design: Bentwood Studio/Jos. Trautwein
Photography: Robert Epstein
Photo Stylist: James Killough

Distributed by Macmillan Publishing Company, a division of Macmillan, Inc.

ISBN 0-02-547650-5
Library of Congress Catalog Card Number: 85-50565

Printed in the United States of America

10 9 8 7 6 5 4 3 2 1

▪FOREWORD▪

The delightful and imaginative wooden toys in this book will bring hours and hours of joy to the lucky children who receive them as gifts. And they will give you the satisfaction that comes with creating simple and sturdy playthings.

A lot of care and love went into this book. Mother Duck waddles around on rubbery feet, as Baby Duck tags along behind . . . and Tuffy Tugboat makes an instant ocean out of the nursery floor.

Most of the toys can be favorites for years and years. As the child grows and begins to put more and more imagination into play, these toys will become an important part of his or her creative development.

Making wooden toys is a traditional American craft you will surely enjoy. We've simplified everything for you—each project has complete step-by-step instructions and easy-to-follow diagrams. We hope *Wooden Toys* brings you all the happiness we put into it.

Gene and Katie Hamilton

CONTENTS

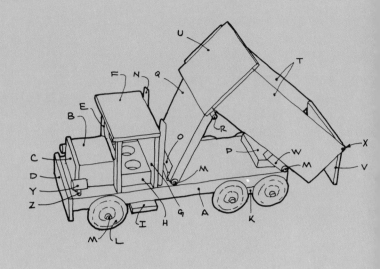

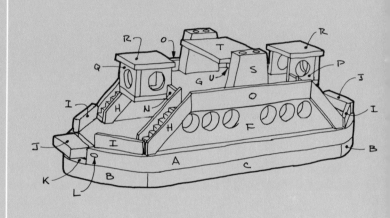

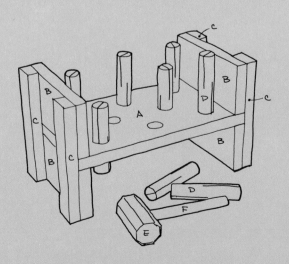

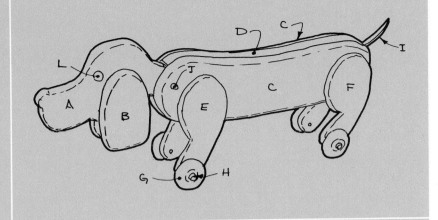

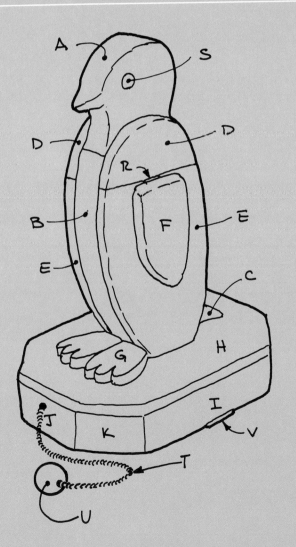

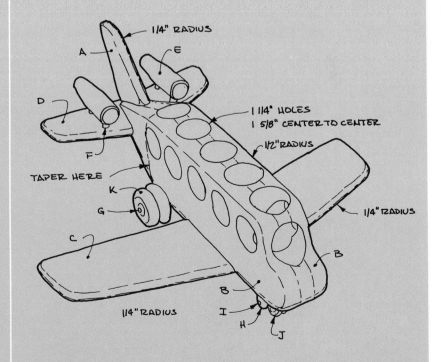

INTRODUCTION

Essentials for the Wooden-Toy Maker

You do not need a shop full of tools to make toys. Most of the designs in this book can be crafted with basic hand tools. Just remember, your child will not care if the edges are not round or the curves perfect. He will enjoy anything that you take the time to build for him. As you progress through the projects in this book your first attempts might seem crude, but we guarantee they will be loved.

Choosing Wood   Traditional craftsmen would choose hardwoods for the projects in this book, but we designed most of the toys so you can construct them using either hard or soft woods.

For many projects we chose pine because it is the most available and economical wood; it is also lightweight and easy to work with using hand tools. Pine is also easy to sand and shape by hand. We suggest you begin with pine then, after completing a project or two, move on to the hardwoods. Feel free to substitute a different wood or use pine for some of the projects we made from birch, maple, or walnut.

To make construction easy, each toy has a shopping and parts list. Most lumberyards stock ¾"-, ½"-, and ¼"-thick wood. Boards that are ¾" thick are available in the common lumber grades and are usually referred to as "one-by" stock, for example, 1 × 6 or 1 × 8. Thinner ½" stock is usually available only in clear grades and is used for trim. And ¼"-thick pine is called lattice and comes in varying widths.

Remember, when working with hardwoods, you must drill pilot holes for all nails and screws. On some projects the edges are rounded over or radiused a quarter of an inch or more; this is best done with a router. Sanding a large radius on the edge of a maple or birch part is just about impossible. But for most projects, easing the sharp corners is all that is necessary.

We recommend that you glue all joints. After the glue has dried, remove the excess with a sharp chisel. Don't skip this step: glue left on the wood will show when you stain or finish the toy.

To prevent splinters, always sand your work. Sand end grain, especially on corners that have been rounded over.

Designed to Be Easy

We designed the toys in this book for ready-made wheels and axles that can be purchased through mail-order sources. We list mail-order sources for toy parts and supplies as well as for woodworking supplies on page 11.

Some of our toys are scaled to fit colorful plastic Little People, which can be purchased at most toy stores. Other toys are designed to fit Matchbox- or Hot Wheel–scale cars and trucks.

Enlarging a Pattern

We give patterns for many of the toys to help in the making of the curved parts. All patterns are drawn on grids made up of 1" squares.

The "passengers" used in many of the toys are a good example of how easy it is to enlarge a pattern. And brown wrapping paper is the best pattern material.

On the brown paper, use a marker to draw 1" squares matching those on the grid pattern. (In our example, the grid is a 3" square.)

In pencil carefully draw the exact lines that you see in the book on each square. Work from square to square until you have the whole pattern drawn on the grid. Go back over the pencil lines and smooth the curves.

Remember, for most parts it is not necessary that they be exactly the same as the pattern. When you are satisfied with the shape, draw over the pencil lines with your marker and cut out the pattern.

Tape the pattern to the wood and trace its shape. The easiest way to locate a hole or eye on the wood is by driving a nail set or awl through the center mark of the hole on the pattern. This transfers the location to the wood.

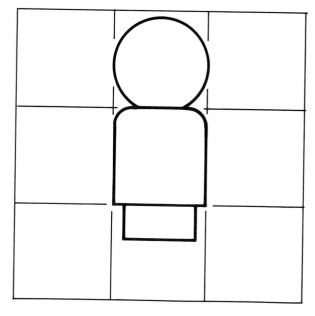

Little People Pattern

Finishing Tips

Finishing Tips   We like a natural wood finish, so on most of the toys we used an easy-to-apply wipe-on finish such as mineral oil or tung oil. For some of the toys we wanted a high-gloss finish so we used varnish. Sand the toy parts before applying a finish and follow the directions provided by the manufacturer.

For the toys requiring a colorful paint job we chose a lead-free oil-based enamel. When you paint, always apply a primer coat first and sand in between coats.

Sandpaper Selection Chart

Use	Grit	Description
Rough sanding	80	Medium
Preparatory sanding	100–120	Fine
Finish sanding		Very Fine
	220–280	Extra-Fine

Safety in the Workshop

Safety in the Workshop   Toy making is easy and rewarding, but be mindful you are working with sharp tools. Always wear eye protection when using any striking tool such as a hammer or power tool.

MAIL-ORDER SOURCES

FOR TOY PARTS:

Cherry Tree Toys, Inc., Belmont, OH 43718.

Craftsman Wood Service Co., 1735 W. Cortland Ct., Addison, IL 60101.

The Toymaker Supply Co., 2907 Lake Forests Rd., Box 5459, Tahoe City, CA 95730.

Toys and Joys, Box 628, Lynden, WA 98264.

The Woodworkers Store, 21801 Industrial Blvd., Rogers, MN 55374.

FOR WOODWORKING SUPPLIES:

Armor Products, Box 290, Deer Park, NY 11729.

Brookstone Co., 127 Vose Farm Rd., Peterborough, NH 03458.

Constantine, 2050 Eastchester Rd., Bronx, NY 10461.

The Fine Tool Shops, Inc., 20 Backus Ave., Danbury, CT, 06810.

Leichtung, Inc., 4944 Commerce Pkway, Cleveland, OH 44128.

Woodcraft, 41 Atlantic Ave., Box 4000, Woburn, MA 01888.

Woodworker's Supply of New Mexico, 5604 Alameda N.E., Albuquerque, NM 87113.

TRAIN

Guaranteed to light up the face of any little engineer, this train will become a collector's item handed down as a family treasure. The rugged little engine pulls a flatcar and three-decker car carrier followed by a spunky caboose. Designed for Matchbox-scale cars, the hardwood train has clean, uncluttered lines with all edges rounded. More than one generation will enjoy the thumps and bumps, knocks and clunks of everyday play with this train.

Shopping List

Quantity	Description
6 feet	1 × 4 pine
2 feet	½″ × 4″ pine
12 feet	¼″ × 4″ pine
1 foot	⅜″ hardwood dowel
1 foot	¼″ hardwood dowel
32	1¼″ dia. × ⅜″ hardwood wheels
32	⁷⁄₃₂″ dia. × 1¼″ axle pegs
1	½″ button plug
3	⅜″ button plug
2	¼″ button plug

BEGIN CONSTRUCTION with the engine. Make the cab (1D) and engine (1E) by gluing pieces of ¾″ stock together, then cut the parts to shape. Cut the frame (1A) from ¾″ stock and the floor (1C) from ½″ stock. Make the wheel blocks (1B), couplings (1H), coupling block (1I), and windows (1M) from ¼″ stock.

Bevel the top edges of the cab, the front and side edges of the engine, and cut the corners off the floor according to the plan. Lay out and drill two ⅜″ holes for the stacks (1F1) in the top of the engine, then mark and drill the headlight (1L) hole in the front of the engine.

Glue the frame and wheel blocks together, then lay out and drill the ⁷⁄₃₂″ holes for the axle pegs in this assembly. Glue the cab and engine to the top of the floor and the frame assembly to the bottom of the floor.

Make the stacks from ⅜″ dowel stock and glue them to the engine. Cut the rails (1N) from ¼″ stock. Bevel their front ends and glue them to the engine sides. Glue the windows to the sides of the cab and the coupling to the front of the floor. The rear coupling is made up of a coupling block and coupling. Glue this assembly to the rear of the floor.

Finish off your engine by gluing the stack caps, which are hardwood button plugs, to the top of the stacks. Drill ¼″ holes in the couplings for the coupling pin (1G). Glue this pin into the hole in the front coupling, then place the wheels (1J) on the axle pegs (1K) and glue them into the holes in the wheel blocks. Make sure the wheels turn freely.

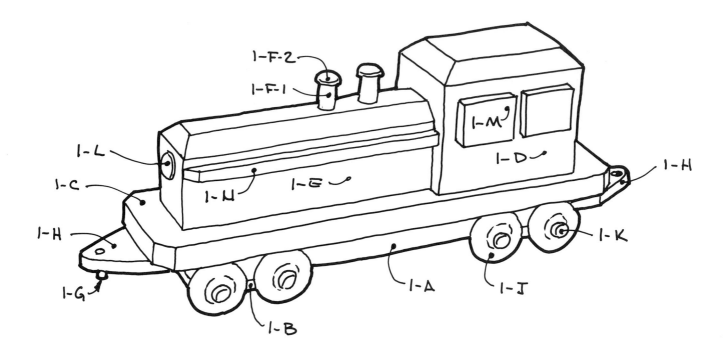

Parts List—**ENGINE**

Part	Name	No.	Size	Material
1A	Frame	1	¾" × 1¾" × 9"	pine
1B	Wheel blocks	2	¼" × 1¾" × 2¼"	pine
1C	Floor	1	½" × 2¾" × 11"	pine
1D	Cab	1	2¼" × 3" × 3½"	pine
1E	Engine	1	1½" × 2" × 5¾"	pine
1F1	Stacks	2	⅜" dia. × 1"	hardwood dowel
1F2	Stack caps	2	⅜" dia.	button plug
1G	Coupling pin	1	¼" dia. × ½"	hardwood dowel
1H	Couplings	2	¼" × 1¾" × 2¼"	pine
1I	Coupling block	1	¼" × 1¾" × 1"	pine
1J	Wheels	8	1¼" dia. × ⅜"	hardwood wheel
1K	Axle pegs	8	7⁄32" dia. × 1¼"	axle peg
1L	Headlight	1	½" dia.	button plug
1M	Windows	4	¼" × 1" × 1¼"	pine
1N	Rails	2	¼" × ¼" × 5¾"	pine

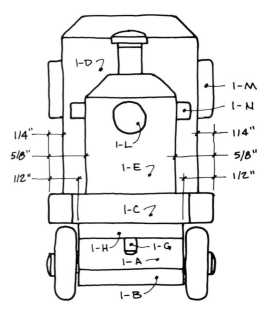

FRONT VIEW

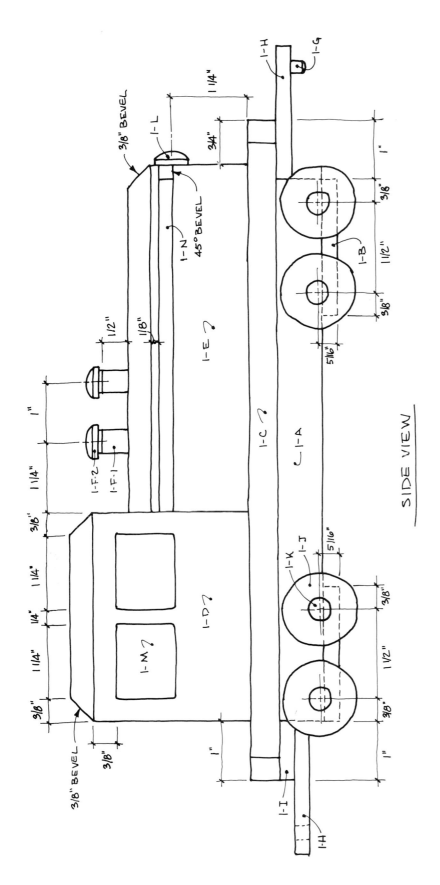

SIDE VIEW

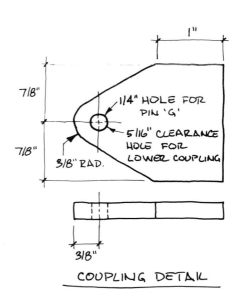

COUPLING DETAIL

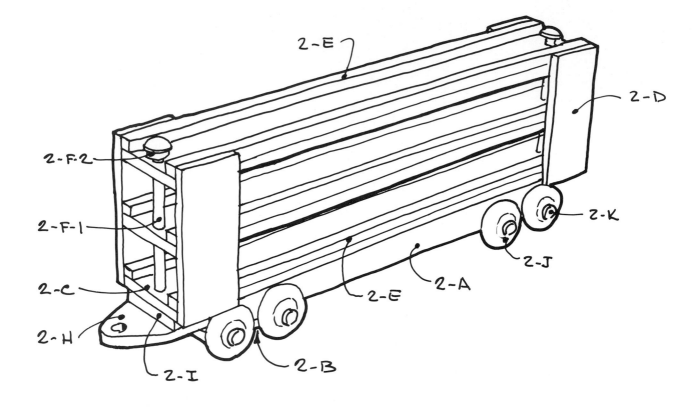

The Car Carrier
and Flatcar

The car carrier and flat car are constructed in the same way. Begin construction of the car carrier by cutting the frame (2A) from ¾″-thick stock. Make the wheel blocks (2B), floors (2C), sides (2D), curbs (2E), and coupling parts (2H) and (2I) from ¼″-thick lattice.

Make the three floor assemblies by gluing the sides to the floor. Drill a ⁵⁄₁₆″ hole near the ends of these assemblies for the locking bars (2F1). Make these bars by gluing ⅜″-dia. caps to the ends of ¼″ dowels.

Glue the wheel blocks to the bottom of one frame assembly and when the glue has set lay out and drill the ⁷⁄₃₂″ axle peg holes. Glue a coupling block

and coupling to one end for the floor and a single coupling to the other.

Assemble the base and the two upper floor assemblies by gluing all three to sides. Lay the car on a flat surface and check that the ends of each floor are flush with the edges of the sides.

When the glue has dried drill ¼″ holes in the couplings for the coupling pin (2G). Glue one pin into the high coupling (the one without the coupling block). Place the wheels (2J) on the axle pegs (2K) and glue them into the holes in the wheel blocks. Check that the wheels turn freely.

The construction of the flatcar follows the same steps as that of the car carrier as the lower units of each are

identical. The only different parts are the trailer block (3F), which is cut from ¾″ stock, and curbs (3E), made from ¼″ lattice.

Make the base the same as the car carrier, then glue the curb to the center of the floor. Glue the trailer block to the curb so it is flush with one end. Drill a ¼″ hole in the trailer block to receive the hitch pin of your trailer.

We finished the train with a wipe-on oil. When the finish has dried, load up the Matchbox-type cars and your truck transport (page 30) for some cross-country hauling fun.

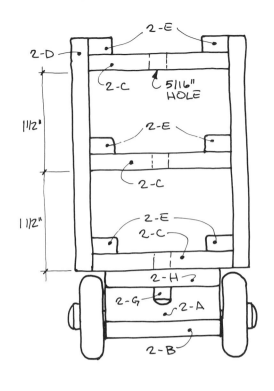

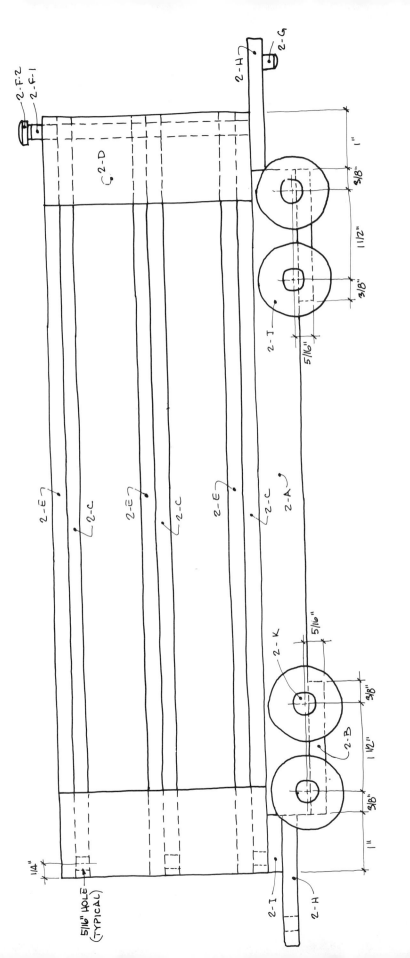

5/16" HOLE (TYPICAL)

Parts List—CAR CARRIER

Part	Name	No.	Size	Material
2A	Frame	1	3/4" × 1 3/4" × 1 -"	pine
2B	Wheel blocks	2	1/4" × 1 3/4" × 2 1/4"	pine
2C	Floors	3	1/4" × 2 1/8" × 13"	pine
2D	Sides	4	1/4" × 1 1/2" × 3 1/2"	pine
2E	Curbs	6	1/4" × 3/8" × 13"	pine
2F1	Locking bars	2	1/4" dia. × 3 3/4"	hardwood dowel
2F2	Caps	2	3/8" dia.	button plug
2G	Coupling pin	1	1/4" dia. × 1/2"	hardwood dowel
2H	Couplings	2	1/4" × 1 3/4" × 2 1/4"	pine
2I	Coupling block	1	1/4" × 1 3/4" × 1"	pine
2J	Wheels	8	1 1/4" dia. × 3/8"	hardwood wheel
2K	Axle pegs	8	3/32" dia. × 1 1/4"	axle peg

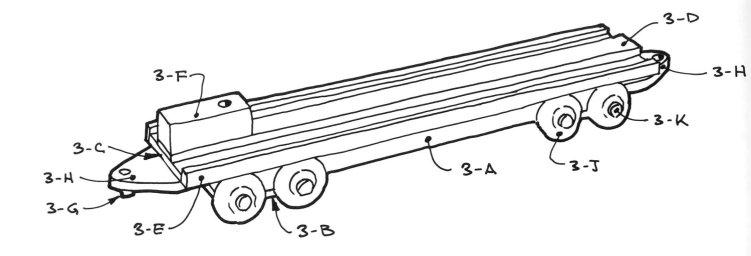

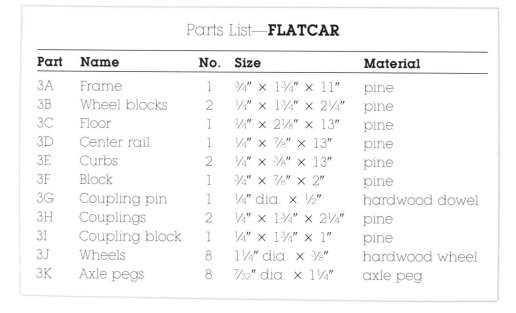

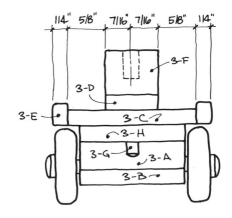

END VIEW

Parts List—**FLATCAR**

Part	Name	No.	Size	Material
3A	Frame	1	¾″ × 1¾″ × 11″	pine
3B	Wheel blocks	2	¼″ × 1¾″ × 2¼″	pine
3C	Floor	1	¼″ × 2⅛″ × 13″	pine
3D	Center rail	1	¼″ × ⅞″ × 13″	pine
3E	Curbs	2	¼″ × ⅜″ × 13″	pine
3F	Block	1	¾″ × ⅞″ × 2″	pine
3G	Coupling pin	1	¼″ dia. × ½″	hardwood dowel
3H	Couplings	2	¼″ × 1¾″ × 2¼″	pine
3I	Coupling block	1	¼″ × 1¾″ × 1″	pine
3J	Wheels	8	1¼″ dia. × ⅜″	hardwood wheel
3K	Axle pegs	8	7/32″ dia. × 1¼″	axle peg

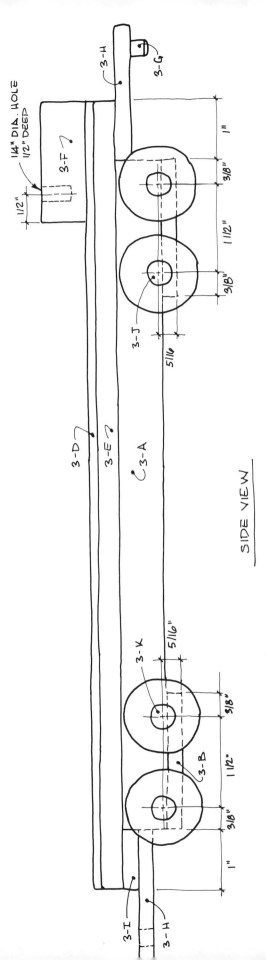

SIDE VIEW

The Caboose

Begin construction of the caboose by gluing up the house (4D) and the front (4E) and rear (4F) houses from pieces of ¾″ stock. Then cut these parts to size. Cut the frame (4A) from ¾″ stock and the floor (4C) from ½″ stock. Make the wheel blocks (4B), couplings (4H), coupling block (4I), windows (4M), and the roof parts (4N), (4O), and (4P) from ¼″ stock.

Glue the frame and wheel blocks together, then lay out and drill the $7/32″$ holes for the axle pegs in this assembly. Glue the house parts to the top of the floor and the frame assembly to the bottom of the floor. Glue the matching roof pieces to the top of the house parts.

Make the stack (4L1) from ⅜″ dowel stock. Lay out and drill its hole in the top of the front house roof, then glue the stack and its cap (4L2) in place. Glue the windows to the sides of the house parts according to the plan.

The front coupling on the caboose is made up of the coupling block and a coupling. Glue this assembly to the front of the floor. Glue a single coupling to the rear. Drill ¼″ holes in the couplings for the coupling pin (4G) and $5/16″$ in lower coupling for clearance. Glue this pin into the hole in the high coupling (the one without the coupling block), then place the wheels (4J) on the axle pegs (4K) and glue them into the holes in the wheel blocks. Check that the wheels turn freely.

Parts List—**CABOOSE**

Part	Name	No.	Size	Material
4A	Frame	1	¾" × 1¾" × 9"	pine
4B	Wheel blocks	2	¼" × 1¾" × 2¼"	pine
4C	Floor	1	½" × 2¾" × 11"	pine
4D	House	1	2¼" × 3 × 3½"	pine
4E	Front house	1	1½" × 2¼" × 2"	pine
4F	Rear house	1	1½" × 2¼" × 3"	pine
4G	Coupling pin	1	¼" dia. × ½"	hardwood dowel
4H	Couplings	2	¼" × 1¾" × 2¼"	pine lattice
4I	Coupling block	1	¼" × 1¾" × 1"	pine lattice
4J	Wheels	8	1¼" dia. × ⅜"	hardwood wheel
4K	Axle pegs	8	⁷⁄₃₂" × 1¼"	axle peg
4L1	Stack	1	⅜" dia. × 1"	hardwood dowel
4L2	Stack cap	1	⅜" dia.	button plug
4M	Windows	10	¼" × 1" × 1¼"	pine lattice
4N	Roof	1	¼" × 2¾" × 4"	pine lattice
4O	Front roof	1	¼" × 2¼" × 2¾"	pine lattice
4P	Rear roof	1	¼" × 2¼" × 4¼"	pine lattice

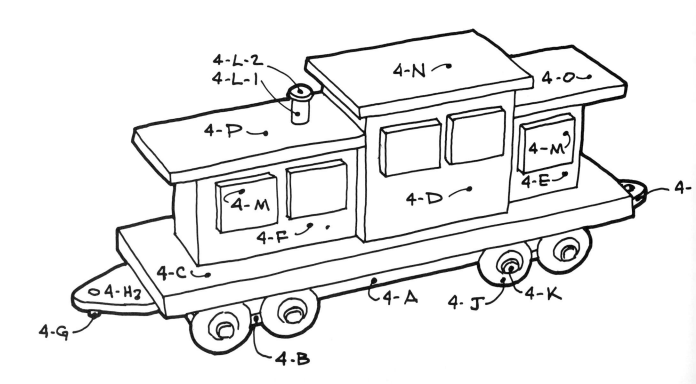

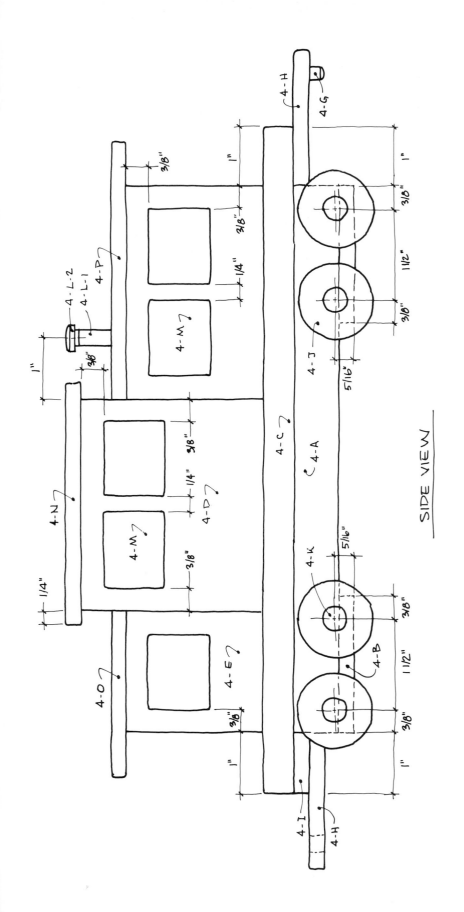

SIDE VIEW

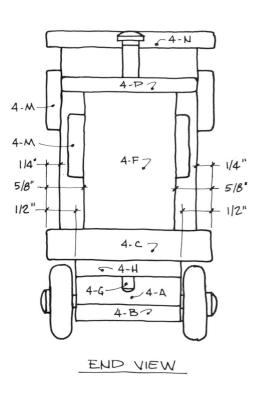

END VIEW

CAR FERRY

Gangplank down . . . all aboard the car ferry! Cars roll up onto the deck of this stout little vessel. Make-believe people can look through porthole windows or walk to the upper deck, which is complete with smokestack and pilothouse on both ends. The ferry rolls along gently on hidden wheels, making it a fun-filled plaything for kids of any age.

BEGIN CONSTRUCTION by making the deck (A). Transfer the deck plan to the pine stock and cut it to shape. Do not cut the front of the deck to a point until after you drill the ¼" holes for ramp hinges (L). Then lay out and cut the ramp notches in each end of the deck.

Cut the two bow/stern (B) parts and hull sides (C) to size. Mark the location and drill ⁷⁄₃₂" holes in the hull sides for the axle pegs. Be sure to allow for wheel clearance when drilling these holes. Insert axle pegs into the wheels and glue them into the holes. Then glue the bow/stern and hull sides to the underside of the deck to form the hull.

Cut the fillers (K) to shape from ¼" lattice and glue them in the notches in the ends of the deck. Sand the deck and hull parts smooth with #120 grit sandpaper.

Lay out the shape of the sides (F) on ¾" pine stock. Cut them to shape with a coping or band saw. Mark the location, then drill the ⅞" portholes. Cut the stacks (S) from this same stock and drill two ½" funnel holes in their tops.

The upper deck (G), stair rails (H), lower rails (I), end rails (N), side rails (O), pilothouse sides (P), pilothouse fronts (Q), pilothouse roofs (R) and shelter roof (T) are cut from ¼" lattice. To prevent splitting the pilothouse pieces when you drill the portholes cut them to width first. Allow for the saw kerfs and lay out the portholes on the lattice strips. Then drill the ⅞" portholes and cut the pieces to size. Rip the center curb (M) and shelter roof supports (U) from ¼" lattice.

Glue pilothouse sides, fronts and roofs to the upper deck according to the plan. Place the sides on a flat surface and glue the upper deck to them. Check to see that the top steps are the same size; this will help align the sides.

Glue all railings to the sides and fit the end rails between the pilothouse and stair rails. Attach the stacks, shelter roof supports, and shelter roof to the upper deck with glue and set the assembly aside to dry.

Form the ½" stock needed for the ramps (J) by gluing two pieces of ¼" lattice together. Round the rear edges of the ramps and place them in position on the bow/stern notches. Use the hinge holes as guides and drill ¼" holes in the edges of the ramps to receive the ramp hinges. Enlarge these holes slightly to allow for easy movement and install the ramps by gluing the ramp hinge dowels in their holes.

Glue the upper deck assembly to the deck according to the pattern, then install the lower rails and center curb with glue.

Finish the ferry naturally with oil or varnish. She is ready to be loaded with Matchbox-type cars for a trip across the lake or the living room.

Shopping List

Quantity	Description
3 feet	1 × 8 pine
3 feet	¼" × 5½" pine
1 foot	¼"-dia. hardwood wheel
4	1"-dia. hardwood wheel
4	⁷⁄₃₂" × 1¼" axle peg

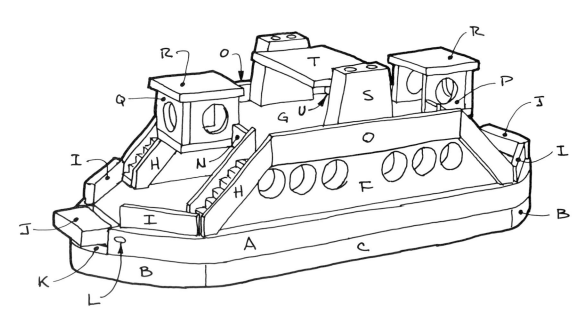

Parts List

Part	Name	No.	Size	Material
A	Deck	1	cut from pattern	pine
B	Bow/stern	2	¾" × 6" × 2¾"	pine
C	Hull sides	2	¾" × 1" × 10½"	pine
D	Wheels	4	1" dia.	hardwood wheel
E	Axle pegs	4	⁵⁄₃₂" × ¹³⁄₁₆"	hardwood peg
F	Sides	2	cut from pattern	pine
G	Upper deck	1	¼" × 5¼" × 10"	pine lattice
H	Stair rails	8	¼" × ⅝" × 3¼"	pine lattice
I	Lower rails	4	¼" × ⅝" × 2¼"	pine lattice
J	Ramps	2	½" × 1⅛" × 2"	pine lattice
K	Fillers	2	cut from pattern	pine lattice
L	Ramp hinges	4	¼" dia. × 1"	hardwood dowel
M	Center curb	1	¼" × ¼" × 7"	pine lattice
N	End rails	4	¼" × ⅝" × ¾"	pine lattice
O	Side rails	2	¼" × ⅞" × 6½"	pine lattice
P	Pilothouse sides	4	¼" × 1¼" × 1½"	pine lattice
Q	Pilothouse fronts	2	¼" × 1¼" × 1¾"	pine lattice
R	Pilothouse roofs	2	¼" × 2" × 2"	pine lattice
S	Stacks	2	cut from pattern	pine
T	Shelter roof	1	¼" × 2½" × 3¾"	pine lattice
U	Shelter roof supports	2	¼" × ¼" × 1⅝"	pine lattice

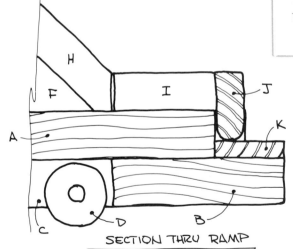

SECTION THRU RAMP

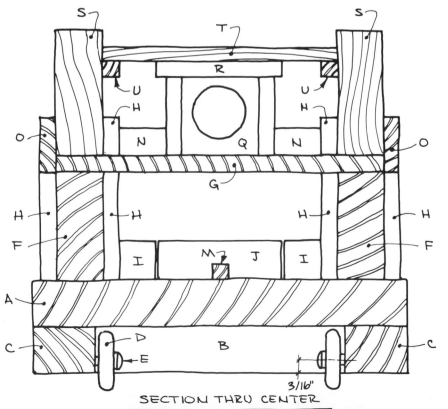

SECTION THRU CENTER

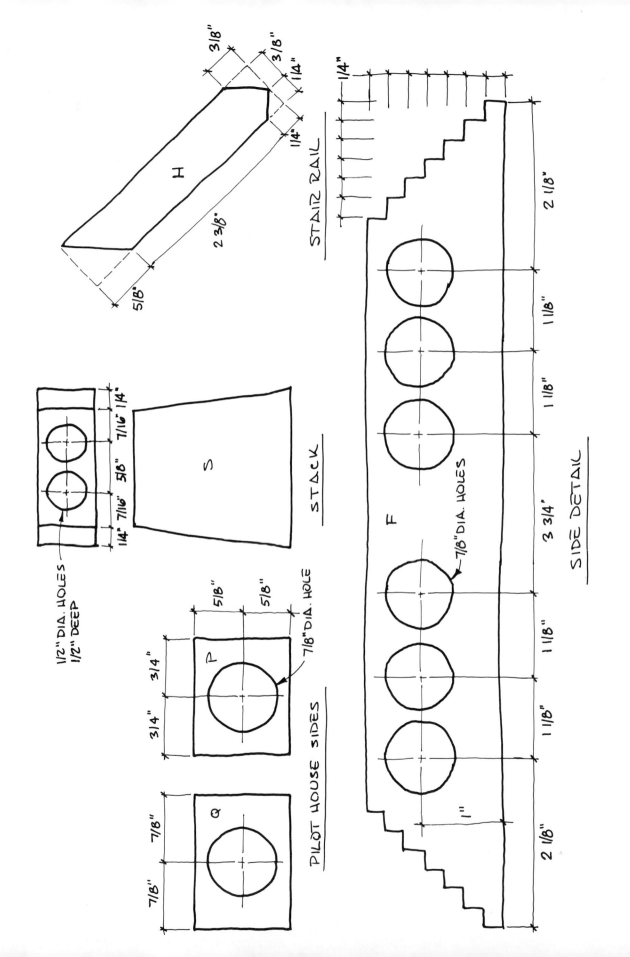

H

3/8" 3/8" 1/4"

1/4"

2 3/8"

5/8"

STAIR RAIL

1/4"

2 1/8"

1 1/8"

1 1/8"

3 3/4"

7/8" DIA. HOLES

F

1 1/8"

1 1/8"

1 1/8"

1"

2 1/8"

SIDE DETAIL

1/4" 7/16"

5/8"

7/16" 1/4"

S

1/2" DIA. HOLES
1/2" DEEP

STACK

5/8" 5/8"

3/4" 3/4"

P

7/8" DIA. HOLE

7/8" 7/8"

Q

PILOT HOUSE SIDES

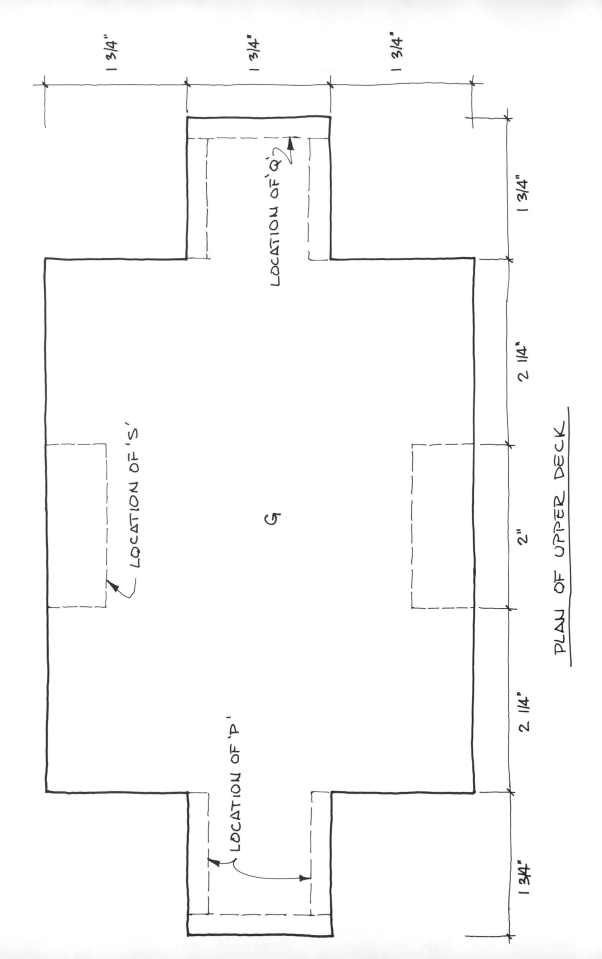

26

LOCATION OF 'Q'

LOCATION OF 'S'

G

LOCATION OF 'P'

1 3/4"

1 3/4"

1 3/4"

1 3/4"

2 1/4"

2"

2 1/4"

1 3/4"

PLAN OF UPPER DECK

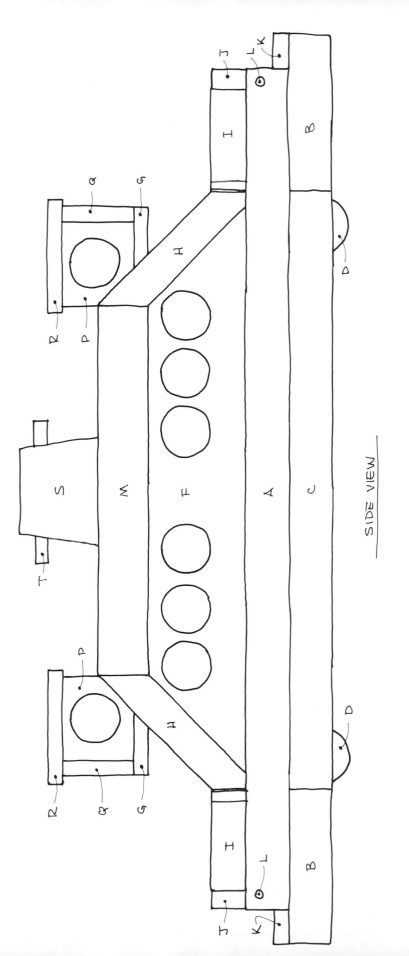

SIDE VIEW

28

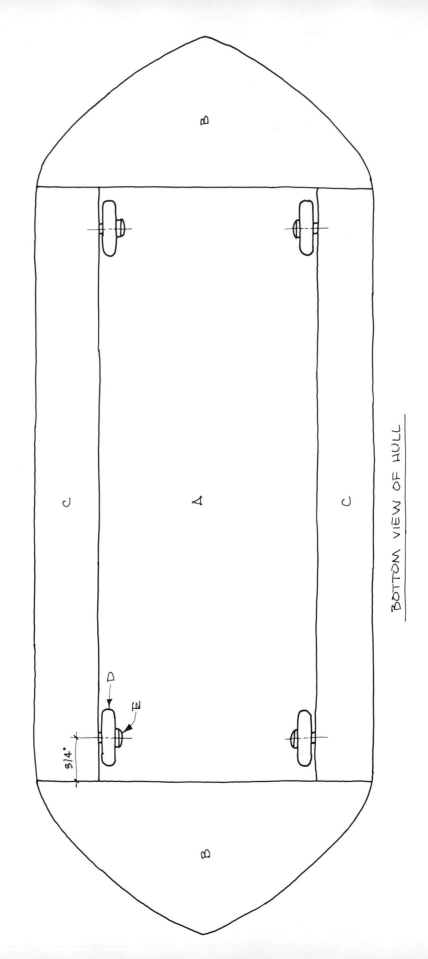

BOTTOM VIEW OF HULL

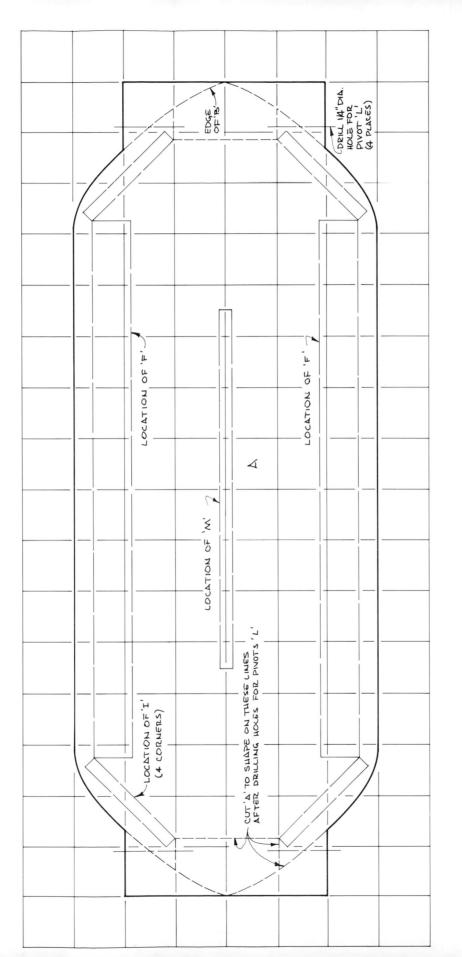

TRUCK TRANSPORT

This husky car hauler is designed for heavy-duty work. Matchbox and Hot Wheel cars roll onto a ramp at the rear of this two-level carrier. The top level pivots downward for easy loading.

Shopping List

Quantity	Description
1 foot	1 × 3 pine
6 feet	¼″ × 1¾″ pine lattice
1 foot	³⁄₁₆″-dia. hardwood dowel
1 foot	¼″-dia. hardwood dowel
6	³⁄₁₆″-dia. axle pegs
2	⅜″-dia. button plugs
18	1″ dia. × ¼″ hardwood wheels
scrap	2 × 4 stock

BEGIN CONSTRUCTION with the tractor. Cut the frame (A) from ¾″-thick stock and make the cab (B) and engine (C) from 2 × 4 stock. Cut the engine skirts (D), cab skirts (E), and bumper (F) from ¼″ pine lattice.

Glue the engine skirts and cab skirts to the frame. Cut the front of the cab to an angle to form the windshield. Sand the cab smooth with #120 grit sandpaper and glue it to the frame with its back edge in alignment with the end of the skirts.

Lay out and drill the holes for the button plug headlights (G) in the front of the engine. Glue these plugs in place, then sand the engine smooth and glue it to the frame.

Lay out and drill three ¼″ holes for the axles (I) in the engine skirts and frame. Drill a ⁵⁄₁₆″ hole in the frame centered between the two rear-drive wheels for the trailer pin (O). Glue one front wheel to its axle, then insert the assembly into the wheel block and glue the other wheel in place. Assemble the rear wheels in the same way, putting two wheels on each side of the axle. Be careful that no glue gets into the axle holes. Check for free wheel movement.

Glue the bumper to the front of the engine and frame, positioning it to be about ¼″ above the floor, and your tractor is ready for hauling.

Begin construction of the trailer by cutting the lower (K) and upper (P) floors, side rails (L), sides (M), cross brace (N), top rails (Q), block (R), curb (S) and links (T) to size from ¼″-thick stock. Make the ramp (V) out of two pieces of ¼″ stock and cut the upper floor supports (U) and trailer pin (O) from ¼″ dowel stock.

Assemble the base of the trailer first. Lay out the position of the hinge pin and in the sides, then drill ³⁄₁₆″ holes through these marks. Also lay out and drill the two ¼″ holes in the wheel block (J) for the axles.

Glue the sides, side rails and cross brace to the lower floor. Hold the ramp in position at the end of the trailer. Use the holes in the side rails as guides when drilling the hinge holes in the ramp. Mark the location of the handle (U) hinge pin hole on the side rails then drill a ³⁄₁₆″ hole through this mark.

Glue the wheels and axles into the wheel block, then glue the wheel block to the bottom of the lower floor. Glue the hinge pins into the ramp. Be careful not to get glue into the holes in the side rails.

(W) holes in the ends of the side rails

Assemble the ramp by gluing the curb to the top of the upper floor and the block to the bottom. Both of these pieces should be flush with the end of the floor. When the glue has dried put this unit in position against the sides. Align it with the front and top edges of the sides and drill a ³⁄₁₆″ hole for the hinge pin.

Temporarily insert the hinge pin into this hole to hold the upper floor assembly in place. Glue the top rails to the sides of the upper floor after aligning them with the sides. Check that there is sufficient clearance between the top rails and side for the upper floor to drop down.

Attach the links to the sides of the lower floor with glue and hinge pins. Glue the handle in place and check that the link assemblies are straight before the glue dries.

Sand notches in the lower edges of the top rails so the top floor assembly rests flat on the upper floor support. Grind the notches until the upper and lower floors are parallel. Glue the hinge pins to the upper floor assembly, and your transport truck is ready to roll.

We finished the pine with an easy-to-apply oil finish.

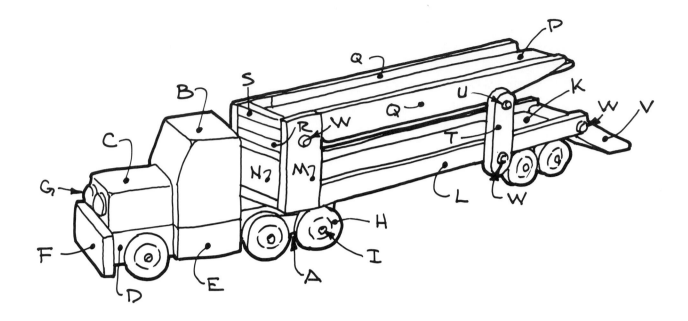

Parts List

Part	Name	No.	Size	Material
A	Frame	1	¾" × 1" × 5½"	pine
B	Cab	1	1½" × 2" × 2"	pine
C	Engine	1	1½" × 1½" × 1"	pine
D	Engine skirts	2	¼" × ¾" × 3"	pine
E	Cab skirts	2	¼" × ¾" × 1½"	pine
F	Bumper	1	¼" × 1" × 2¼"	pine
G	Headlights	2	⅜" dia.	button plug
H	Wheels	18	1" dia. × ¼"	hardwood wheel
I	Axles	5	3⁄16" dia. × 2"	hardwood dowel
J	Wheel block	1	¾" × 1" × 2¼"	pine
K	Lower floor	1	¼" × 1½" × 10"	pine
L	Side rails	2	¼" × ½" × 9½"	pine
M	Sides	2	¼" × 1" × 2¼"	pine
N	Cross brace	1	¼" × 1" × 1½"	pine
O	Trailer pin	1	¼" dia. × ⅝"	hardwood dowel
P	Upper floor	1	¼" × 1½" × 10¼"	pine
Q	Top rails	2	¼" × ¾" × 8½"	pine
R	Block	1	¼" × 1" × 1½"	pine
S	Curb	1	¼" × ¼" × 1½"	pine
T	Links	2	¼" × ¾" × 2¼"	pine
U	Upper floor support	1	¼" dia. × 3"	hardwood dowel
V	Ramp	1	½" × 1½" × 3"	pine
W	Hinges	6	5⁄32" dia. × 13⁄16"	axle peg

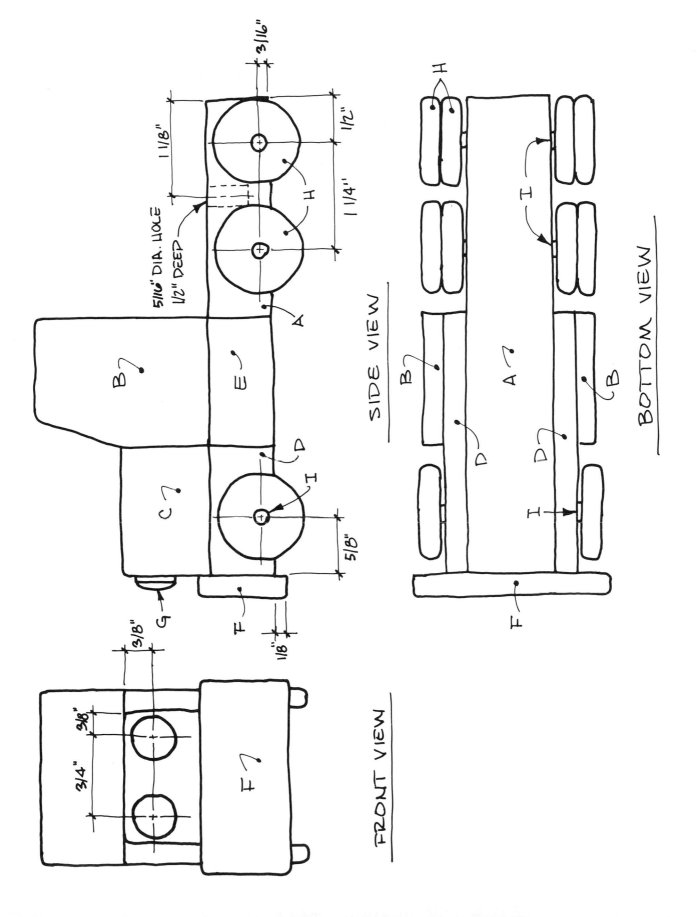

33

FRONT VIEW

SIDE VIEW

BOTTOM VIEW

34

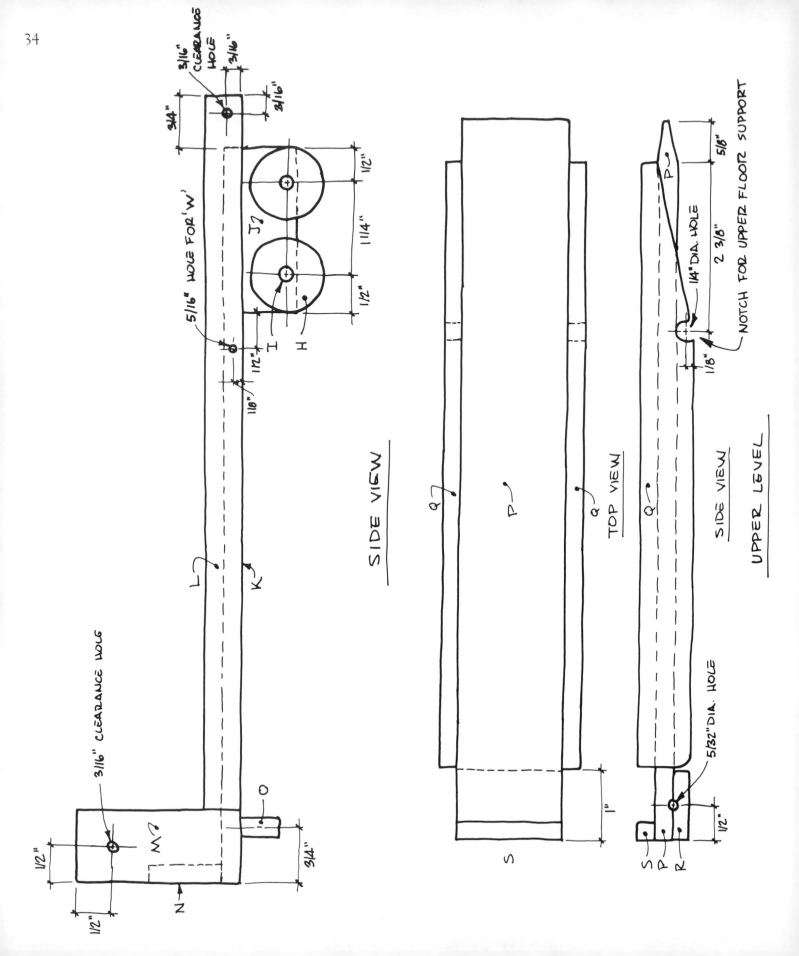

3/16" CLEARANCE HOLE

3/16"

3/4"

3/16"

1/2"

J

1 1/4"

1/2"

5/16" HOLE FOR 'W'

I

H

1/2"

1/8"

L

K

3/16" CLEARANCE HOLE

1/2"

M

O

N

3/4"

1/2"

SIDE VIEW

Q

P

Q

TOP VIEW

S

1"

P

5/8"

2 3/8"

1/4" DIA. HOLE

NOTCH FOR UPPER FLOOR SUPPORT

1/8"

Q

SIDE VIEW

5/32" DIA. HOLE

S

P

R

1/2"

UPPER LEVEL

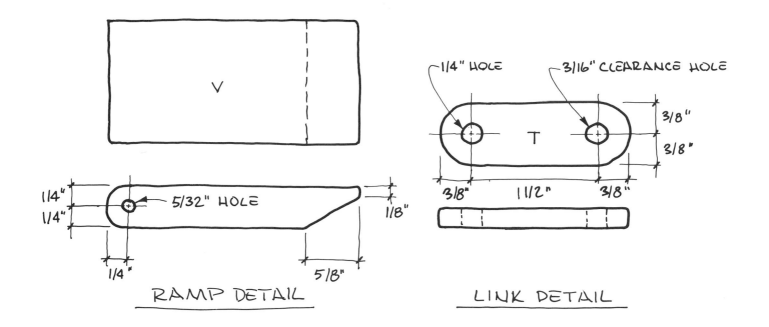

V

5/32" HOLE

1/4"
1/4"

1/4"

5/8"

1/8"

RAMP DETAIL

1/4" HOLE

3/16" CLEARANCE HOLE

T

3/8"

3/8"

3/8"

1 1/2"

3/8"

LINK DETAIL

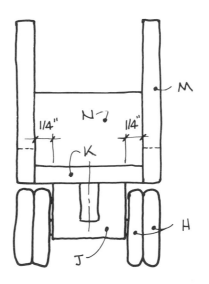

M

1/4"

N

1/4"

K

H

J

FRONT VIEW

FIRE ENGINE

Here's an old-fashioned hook-'n'-ladder fire truck with a four-section ladder that can climb to the sky—well, almost! The engine cab pulls the carrier with a base that holds the ladders. This truck can withstand the knocks and clunks of your little fire chief's everyday play.

BEGIN CONSTRUCTION of the cab by cutting the cab frame (A) and engine (B) from ¾" pine stock. Cut the seats (E) from ½"-thick pine, then make the rear (C) and front (D) wheel blocks, doors (F), cab back (G), windshield base (H), and bumper (I) from ¼" pine lattice.

Glue the engine to the top of the cab frame flush with its front. Glue the front and rear wheel blocks to the bottom of the cab frame flush with the ends. Lay out, then drill, the two ⅞" holes for the firemen in the seats (E).

Shopping List

Quantity	Description
2 feet	1 × 3 pine
6 feet	¼" × 2½" pine lattice
6 feet	¼"-dia. hardwood dowel
10	1¼"-dia. hardwood wheels
10	⁷⁄₃₂" dia. × 1¼" axle peg
2	⅜"-dia. button plug

Parts List

Part	Name	No.	Size	Material
A	Cab frame	1	¾" × 2¼" × 6½"	pine
B	Engine	1	¾" × 2¼" × 1¾"	pine
C	Rear wheel blocks	2	¼" × 2¼" × 2¾"	pine lattice
D	Front wheel block	1	¼" × 2¼" × 1¼"	pine lattice
E	Seats	3	½" × 1½" × 2¼"	pine
F	Doors	2	¼" × 1¾" × 2"	pine lattice
G	Cab back	1	¼" × 2¼" × 2¼"	pine lattice
H	Windshield base	1	¼" × ¼" × 2¼"	pine lattice
I	Bumper	1	¼" × 1¼" × 3¼"	pine lattice
J	Wheels	10	1¼" dia. × ⅜"	hardwood wheel
K	Axles	10	⁷⁄₃₂" dia. × 1¼"	hardwood peg
L	Trailer frame	1	¾" × 2¼" × 12½"	pine
M	Sides	2	¼" × 1½" × 15½"	pine lattice
N	Floor	1	¼" × 2¼" × 15½"	pine lattice
O	Trailer peg	1	¼" dia. × ½"	hardwood peg
P	Ladder sides	8	¼" × ½" × 11½"	pine lattice
Q	Ladder rungs	12	¼" dia. × 1½"	hardwood dowel
R	Ladder rungs	20	¼" dia. × 2"	hardwood dowel
S	Headlights	2	⅜" dia.	hardwood button

Glue this part to the cab frame just behind the engine.

Glue the cab back to the rear of the seat, then glue the doors and windshield base in place. On the side of the cab frame mark the location and drill the 7/32" holes for axles (K). Lay out and drill 5/16" hole in the cab frame to receive the trailer peg. Mark and drill two 3/8" holes for the headlights (S) in the front of the engine. Glue a 3/8" button plug into each of these holes.

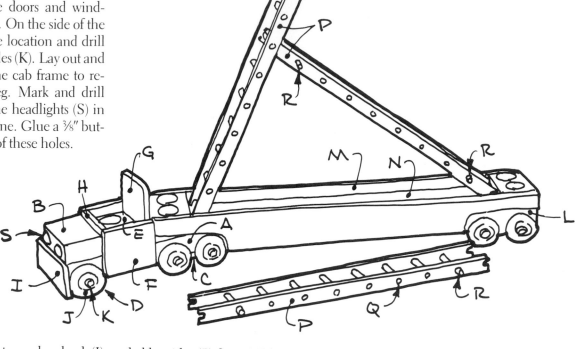

Insert an axle into each wheel (J) and then glue the axles to the cab frame, checking that all wheels move freely. Finish the cab by gluing the bumper in place.

To make the ladder trailer cut the trailer frame (L) from 3/4"-thick stock. Make the sides (M) by transferring their basic shape from the plan to 1/4"-thick lattice, then cut them to shape. Cut the floor (N) from the same stock.

Glue the wheel block to the bottom of the trailer frame and the floor to the top flush with its end. Glue a seat to each end of the floor, then glue on the sides.

After the glue has dried, round the front corners of the trailer according to the plan. Drill a 1/4" hole in the underside of the floor for the trailer peg, then glue it in place. Lay out and drill the 7/32" axle holes in the side of the frame. Insert the axles into the wheels and glue them into these holes. Check that the wheels move freely.

The ladders can be built quickly if you make the sides in pairs. Cut the ladder sides (P) from 1/4" lattice. Make them about an inch longer than necessary. Stack them on top of one another when drilling the 1/4" rung holes. After you have drilled all the rung holes, cut the sides to final length by cutting through the center of the end rung hole.

Cut the long (Q) and short (R) rungs from the 1/4" dowel stock. Assemble the narrow ladders first. Glue the long rungs into the first and last rung holes of a ladder side so that they protrude a quarter of an inch. This provides a stud for the end of the wide ladder to fit over. Glue the short rungs into the remaining rung holes, then glue the other ladder side in place. Construct the wide ladder the same way, using only long rungs. Place all the ladders on a flat surface to dry.

Apply an oil finish, and your hook-'n'-ladder truck is ready to roll. We used store-bought firemen, but you can turn your own from the pattern provided in the introduction (p. 9).

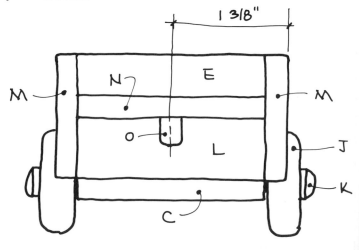

END VIEW

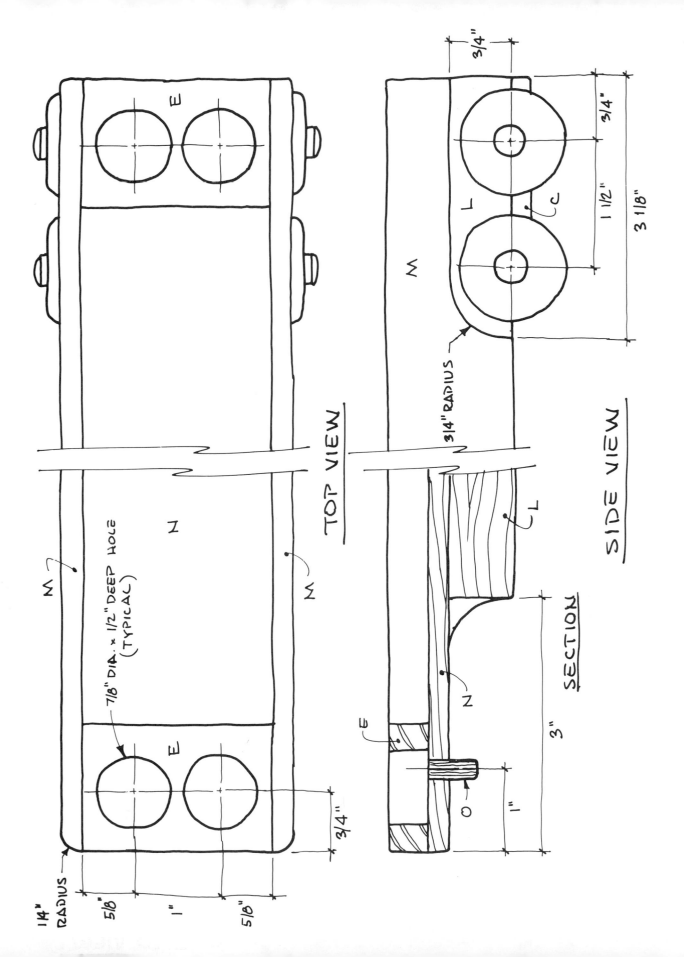

TOP VIEW

SIDE VIEW

SECTION

M

N

E

E

M

M

L

C

L

N

O

14" RADIUS

5/8"

1"

5/8"

3/4"

7/8" DIA. × 1/2" DEEP HOLE (TYPICAL)

3/4"

3/4"

1 1/2"

3 1/8"

3/4" RADIUS

3"

1"

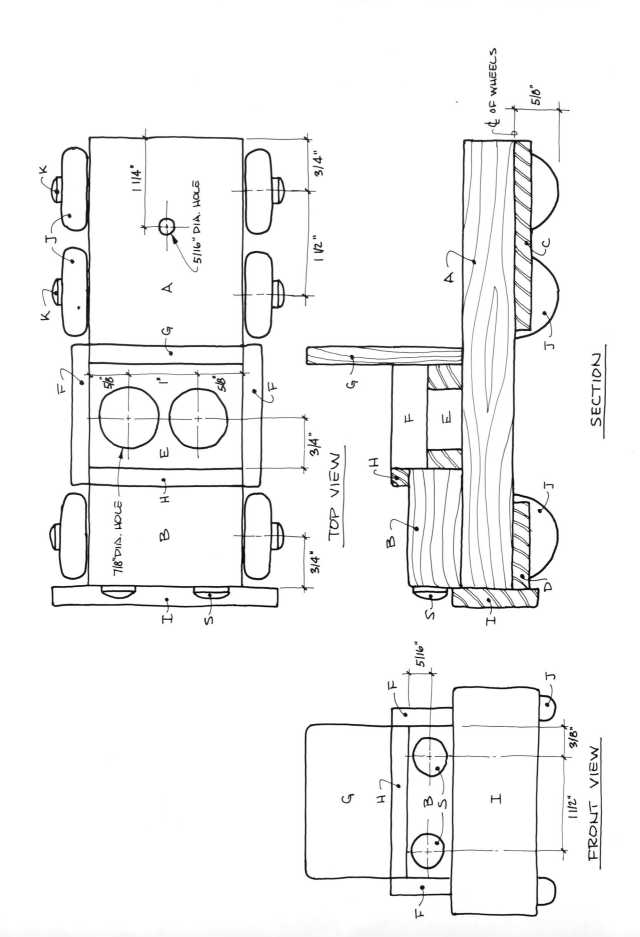

5/16" DIA. HOLE

1 1/4"

3/4"

1 1/2"

K

J

A

G

F

5/8

1"

5/8

E

H

B

F

7/8" DIA. HOLE

3/4"

3/4"

I

S

TOP VIEW

℄ OF WHEELS

5/8"

A

C

J

G

F

E

H

B

J

D

S

I

SECTION

5/16"

F

G

H

B

S

3/8"

I

J

1 1/2"

F

FRONT VIEW

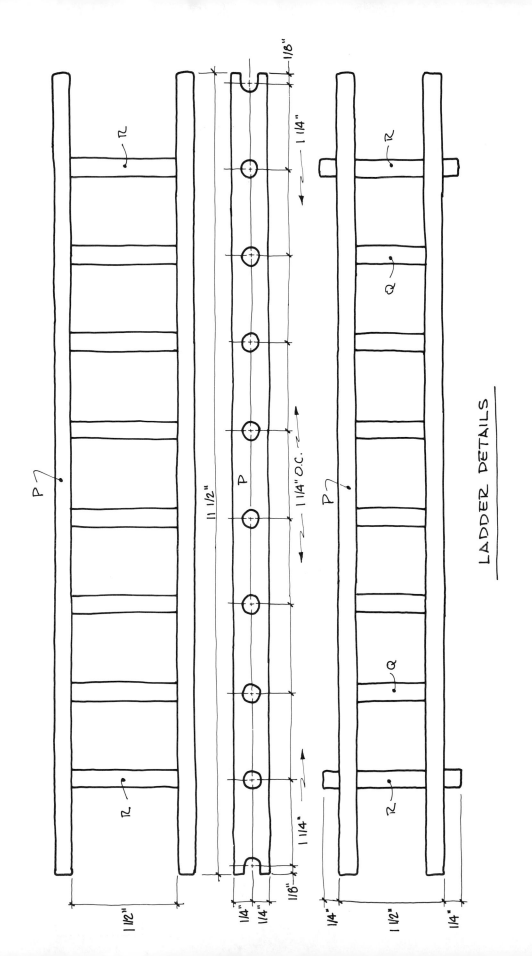

1/8"

R

1 1/4"

R

11 1/2"

P

Q

P

1 1/4" O.C.

P

Q

1 1/2"

1 1/4"

R

R

1/8"

1/4"
1/4"

1/4"
1 1/2"
1/4"

LADDER DETAILS

DUMP TRUCK

It's a hardworking, heavy-duty six-wheeler itching to move! Just like the real thing, the truck box lifts up with a dumping lever and the tailgate swings open. It is easy to build because we use ready-made wheels. The dumpster's cab is designed to carry plastic Little People, or you can make your own.

Shopping List

Quantity	Description
2 feet	1 × 6 pine
1 foot	2 × 4 pine
4 feet	¼″ × 5¼″ pine lattice
2 feet	½″ × 5¼″ pine
1 foot	⅛″-dia. birch dowel
2 feet	¼″-dia. birch dowel
1 foot	½″-dia. birch dowel
6	2″ dia. × ⅞6″ hardwood wheels
10	⁷⁄₃₂″ dia. × 1¼″ axles

BEGIN CONSTRUCTION by making the frame (A) and seat (H) out of ¾″ stock. Shape the hood (B) from 2 × 4 stock or glue it up from two pieces of ¾″ stock. From ¼″ lattice stock make the cab and engine parts: grill (C), bumper (D), cab front (E), roof (F), and cab back (G).

Glue the hood to the frame, taking care to locate it ½″ back from the frame's front edge. To cut out the shape of the windshield on the cab front, drill ¾″ holes in each corner and remove the wood between the holes with a coping or saber saw. Glue the grill to the front of the hood, then glue the cab front to the back of the hood. Use clamps or ⅝″ wire brads to hold the grill and the cab front in place while the glue dries.

Drill two ⅞″ holes in the seat for the

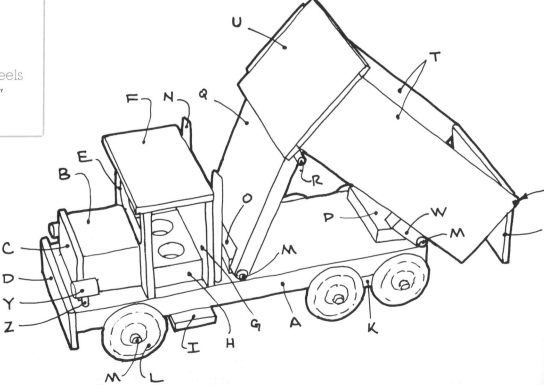

driver and passenger, then glue the seat tight against the cab front. Place the cab back tight against the seat and mark the location of the exhaust pipes (N). Drill ¼″ holes for these pipes before you glue the cab back and roof in place.

Make the headlights (Y) out of ½″ dowel stock. Drill ¼″ holes in the headlights' sides for the light posts (Z) and drill mounting holes in the frame. Sand the headlights to break down all sharp edges and glue them to the light posts. Then glue the assemblies to the truck frame.

Cut the front (J) and rear (K) blocks from ½″ stock. Drill axle holes in their ends, then glue to underside of the frame. Install the wheels and axles by placing a small amount of glue in the axle holes. Check to see that the wheels turn freely before the glue sets. Install the step (I) behind the front wheels.

Make the box bottom (S), dump box pad (P), dump lever (Q), and lever pad (O) out of ½″ stock. The other box parts (T), (U), and (V) are cut from ¼″ stock.

Drill the holes for the hinge pins in

the lever pad, then install it behind the cab. Make matching holes in the dump lever, then apply a small amount of glue to the hinge pin holes of the lever pad and slip the hinge pins in place.

Drill the ⅛″ holes for the tailgate hinges (X) in the tailgate and box sides. Assemble the dump box with glue and ⅝″ wire brads. Check for free movement of the tailgate.

The easiest way to make the dump box pad (P) and hinge blocks (W) is to cut them as one piece. Drill the hinge pin holes about 1¼″ deep in the ends of this block, then cut off the hinge blocks from each end.

Glue the dump box pad flush with the rear of the frame and the hinge blocks to the bottom of the dump box. Check the hinge pin alignment and that the dump box has full travel.

Sand all parts with #220 grit sandpaper. We finished our truck natural with an easy-to-apply wipe-on finish. Our driver and helper are colorful plastic, but you can turn your own from the pattern we included in the Introduction (p. 9).

When the finish has dried, assemble the dump box on the truck and glue in the hinge pins.

Parts List

Part	Name	No.	Size	Material
A	Frame	1	¾" × 3¾" × 11⅞"	pine
B	Hood	1	1½" × 1¾" × 2½"	pine
C	Grill	1	¼" × 1⅝" × 2¾"	pine
D	Bumper	1	¼" × 1⅜" × 4½"	pine
E	Cab front	1	¼" × 3¼" × 3¾"	pine
F	Roof	1	¼" × 2⅜" × 4¼"	pine
G	Cab back	1	¼" × 3¼" × 3¾"	pine
H	Seat	1	¾" × 1⅝" × 2¾"	pine
I	Step	1	¼" × 1¼" × 4¾"	pine
J	Front block	1	½" × 1" × 3¾"	pine
K	Rear block	1	½" × 3¼" × 3¾"	pine
L	Wheels	6	2" dia. × ⁷⁄₁₆"	birch wheel
M	Axle/hinges	10	⁷⁄₃₂" dia. × 1¼"	birch axle
N	Exhaust pipes	2	¼" dia. × 4¼"	birch dowel
O	Lever pad	1	½" × ⅝" × 2¹¹⁄₁₆"	pine
P	Dump box pad	1	½" × 1½" × 2¹¹⁄₁₆"	pine
Q	Dump lever	1	½" × 3¾" × 5¼"	pine
R	Dump handle	1	¼" dia. × 1½"	birch dowel
S	Box bottom	1	½" × 4½" × 7½"	pine
T	Box sides	2	¼" × 2¾" × 8"	pine
U	Box front	1	¼" × 3⅝" × 4½"	pine
V	Tailgate	1	¼" × 2¾" × 4⁷⁄₁₆"	pine
W	Hinge blocks	2	½" × ½" × 1½"	pine
X	Tailgate hinges	2	⅛" dia. × ⅝"	birch dowel
Y	Headlights	2	½" dia. × ¾"	birch dowel
Z	Light posts	2	¼" dia. × ⅞"	birch dowel

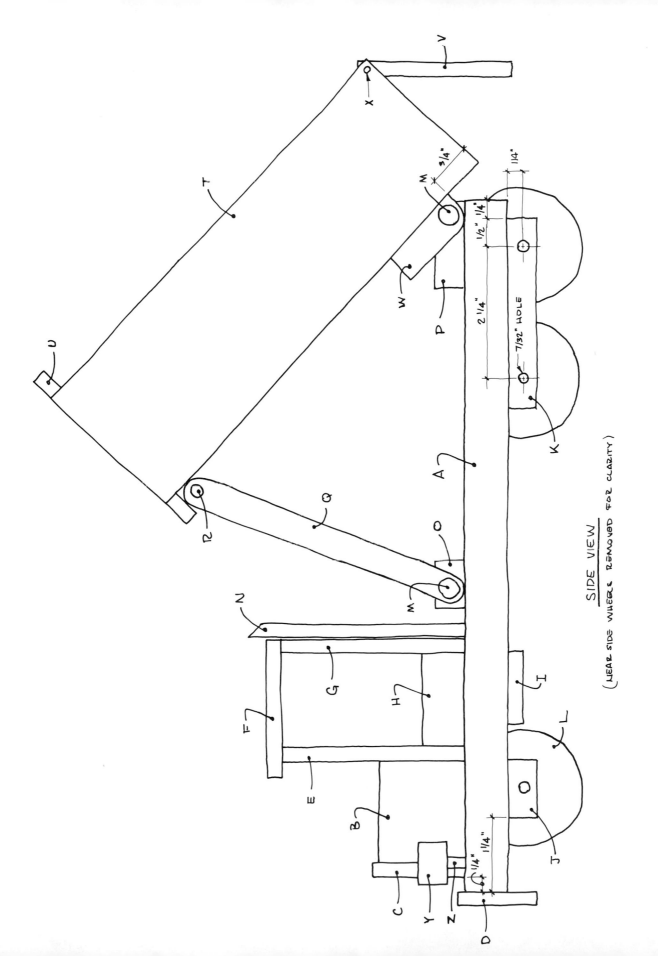

SIDE VIEW
(NEAR SIDE WHEELS REMOVED FOR CLARITY)

45

TOP VIEW

FRONT VIEW

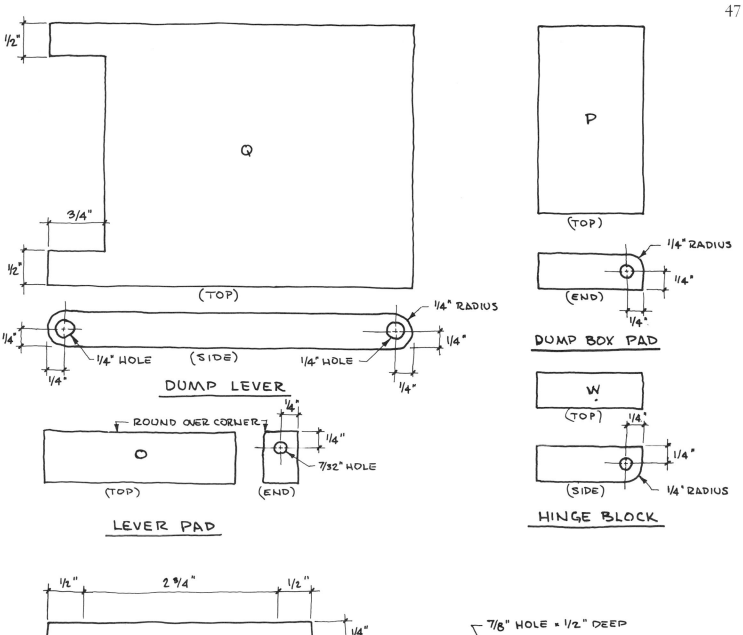

1/2"

3/4"

1/2"

Q

(TOP)

1/4" RADIUS

1/4"

1/4" HOLE   (SIDE)   1/4" HOLE   1/4"

1/4"

DUMP LEVER

ROUND OVER CORNER

1/4"

1/4"

O

7/32" HOLE

(TOP)   (END)

LEVER PAD

P

(TOP)

1/4" RADIUS

1/4"

(END)   1/4"

DUMP BOX PAD

W

(TOP)   1/4"

1/4"

(SIDE)   1/4" RADIUS

HINGE BLOCK

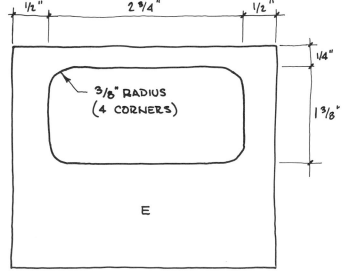

1/2"   2 3/4"   1/2"

1/4"

3/8" RADIUS
(4 CORNERS)

1 3/8"

E

CAB FRONT

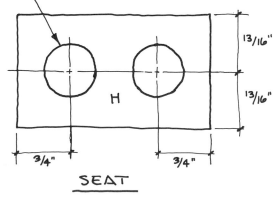

7/8" HOLE × 1/2" DEEP

13/16"

H

13/16"

3/4"   3/4"

SEAT

TUFFY TUGBOAT

Here's a chubby little tug that is sure to win the hearts of everyone who sees it. Our salty tugboat is designed to carry Little People as passengers and crew and is easy to build using only a few tools.

Shopping List

Quantity	Description
4 feet	1 × 8 pine
1 foot	2 × 4 pine
2 feet	1/4″ × 5½″ pine
1 foot	1/8″ hardwood dowel
1 foot	3/16″ hardwood dowel
1 foot	3/8″ hardwood dowel
1 foot	5/8″ hardwood dowel
3	1″ dia. × 1/4″ hardwood wheels

BEGIN CONSTRUCTION by enlarging the pattern for the deck plan and underside of the tug. Transfer your patterns for the hull (A), bows (D2), bow skirt (D1), stern (B) and side skirts (C) to 3/4″ pine stock. Use a band or coping saw to cut these parts to shape.

Lay out and drill the 3/8″ holes for the mooring posts (T) in the deck side of the hull. Glue the stern, side and bow skirts to the underside of the hull.

Glue the two bow pieces (D2) together to form one V. When the glue is dry cut the bow pieces to a taper to match the side view of these parts.

Round their top edges and glue them to the bow of the hull.

Use a sanding disk to shape the skirts and hull into a smooth line. Finish sanding the hull with #120 grit sandpaper and sanding block.

Cut the front (X) and rear (Y) wheel blocks to size and drill 3/16″ holes in their sides for the axles (W). Assemble the wheels (V) and blocks, then glue them to the underside of the hull.

Build the deckhouse over your enlarged deck plan as you would a model. Cut the house fronts (E), house sides (F) and house ends (G) from 1/4″-thick

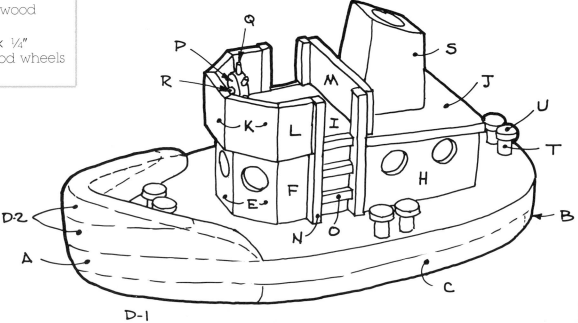

stock. Lay out and drill ¾″ holes for the port lights in the house fronts. Sand 22-degree bevels on the house-front sides. Check the fit of the bevels, then assemble and glue these parts together.

Cut the cabin sides (H) and ends (G) to size, then drill two port lightholes in each piece. Glue these parts to the back of the house assembly.

Make the house roof (I), cabin roof (J) and the bridge front (K), bridge side (L) and bridge back (M) from ¼″ stock.

Drill a ³⁄₁₆″ hole for the wheel column (R) in the center of the bridge front.

Glue the house and cabin roofs in place. When the glue has set, glue the bridge parts to the house front and roof according to the plan. Check that their upper edges are 3¼″ above the deck.

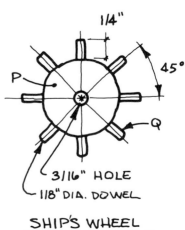

1/4″

45°

P

Q

3/16″ HOLE

118″ DIA. DOWEL

SHIP'S WHEEL

Cut ¼″ stock into ⅜″-wide strips and cut this stock to length to form the ladder sides (N). Make the ladder steps (O) by cutting off ¼″-wide strips from the same stock, then cut these strips to size to form the steps.

Glue the forward ladder side to the side of the house flush with the back of the bridge side. Glue the rear ladder side to the front of the cabin, then glue the ladder steps in place. Glue the bridge back to the rear of the ladder.

Cut the stack (S) from 2 × 4 stock. Drill the 1″ smoke hole in its top before you cut the angle.

Make the mooring posts (T) from ⅜″-dia. dowel stock. Fashion the caps (U) by cutting short sections from a ⅝″-dia. hardwood dowel. Glue the posts into their deck holes, then glue the caps to the top of the posts.

Make the wheel hub (P) by cutting a ¼″-thick slice off a 1″-dia. hardwood dowel. Drill ⅛″ holes in the hub's edge for the wheel spokes (Q), which are cut from ⅛″ dowel stock.

When all glue has dried, finish-sand with #220 grit sandpaper and finish with a wipe-on oil.

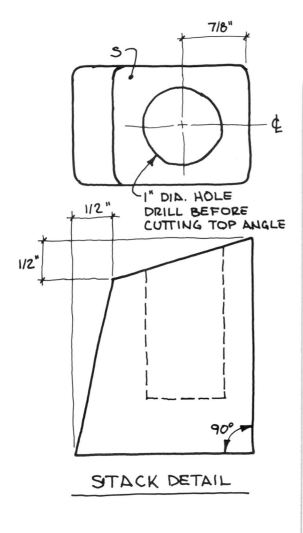

7/8"

S

¢

1" DIA. HOLE DRILL BEFORE CUTTING TOP ANGLE

1/2 "

1/2"

90°

STACK DETAIL

Parts List

Part	Name	No.	Size	Material
A	Hull	1	cut from pattern	pine
B	Stern skirt	1	cut from pattern	pine
C	Side skirts	2	cut from pattern	pine
D1	Bow skirt	1	cut from pattern	pine
D2	Bows	2	cut from pattern	pine
E	House fronts	3	¼″ × 1¼″ × 2″	pine
F	House sides	2	¼″ × 2″ × 2¼″	pine
G	Cabin/house ends	2	¼″ × 1¾″ × 3″	pine
H	Cabin sides	2	¼″ × 2″ × 3½″	pine
I	House roof	1	¼″ × 3″ × 3¼″	pine
J	Cabin roof	1	¼″ × 3¾″ × 3⅝″	pine
K	Bridge fronts	3	¼″ × 1½″ × 1½″	pine
L	Bridge sides	2	¼″ × 7/8″ × 1½″	pine
M	Bridge back	1	¼″ × 1″ × 3½″	pine
N	Ladder sides	4	¼″ × ⅜″ × 3¼″	pine
O	Ladder steps	6	¼″ × ¼″ × 1⅛″	pine
P	Wheel hub	1	¼″ × 1″ dia.	pine
Q	Wheel spokes	8	⅛″ dia. × ½″	hardwood dowel
R	Wheel column	1	3/16″ dia. × ⅝″	hardwood dowel
S	Stack	1	1½″ × 2¼″ × 2¾″	pine
T	Mooring posts	8	⅜″ dia. × 1″	hardwood dowel
U	Caps	8	⅝″ dia. × 3/16″	hardwood dowel
V	Wheels	3	1″ dia. × ¼″	hardwood wheel
W	Axles	3	3/16″ dia. × 1⅜″	hardwood dowel
X	Front blocks	2	¾″ × 1″ × ½″	pine
Y	Rear block	1	¾″ × 1″ × 4″	pine

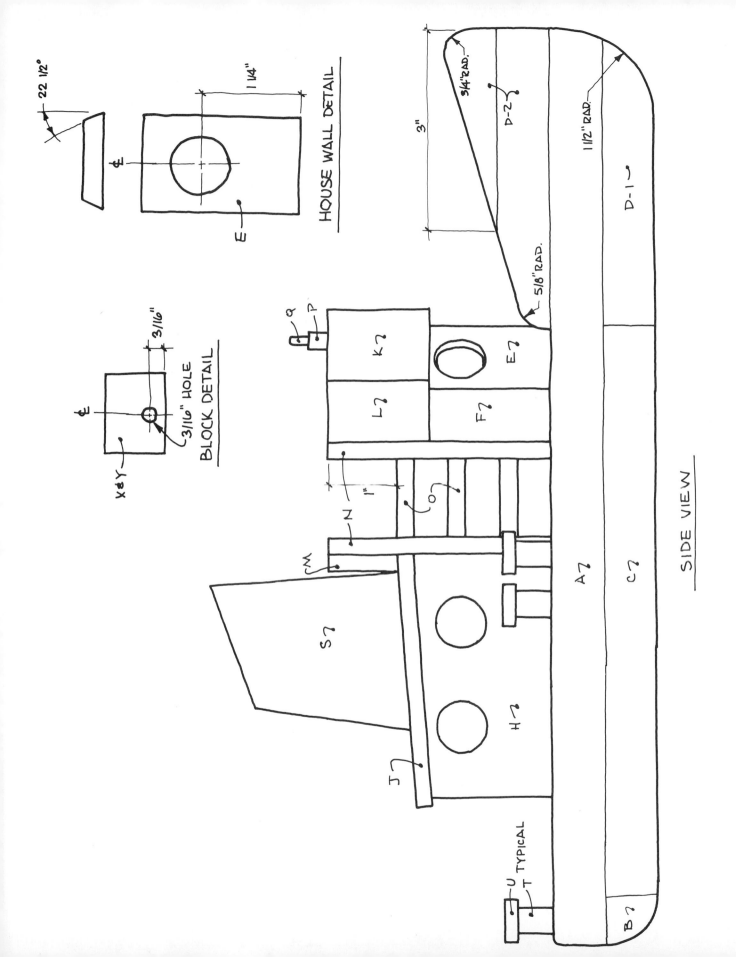

HOUSE WALL DETAIL

22 1/2°

1 1/4"

₵

E

3/16"

₵

3/16" HOLE

X & Y

BLOCK DETAIL

3"

3/4" RAD.

D-2

1 1/2" RAD.

D-1

5/8" RAD.

Q

P

K

L

E

F

N

1"

O

M

S

H

J

A

C

U TYPICAL

T

B

SIDE VIEW

52

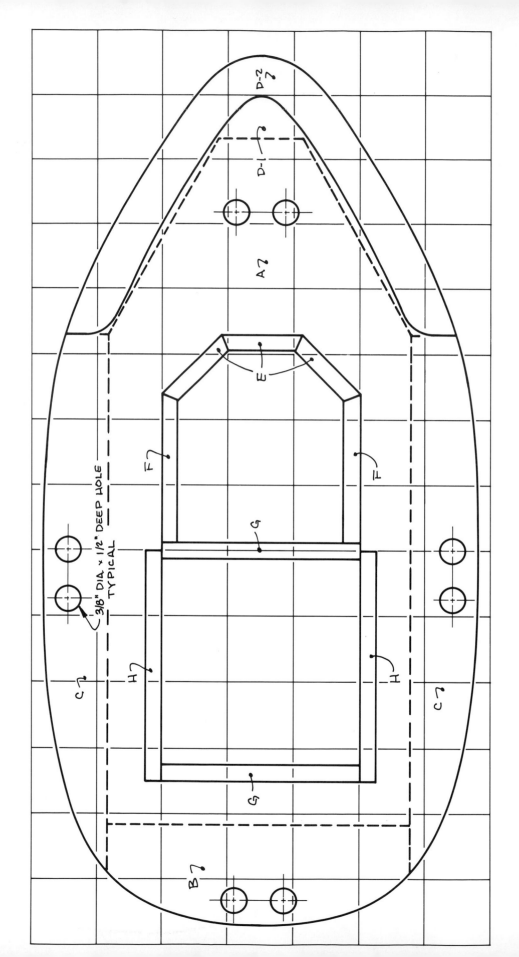

D-2

D-1

A

E

F

F

G

3/8" DIA. × 1/2" DEEP HOLE
TYPICAL

H

H

C

G

C

B

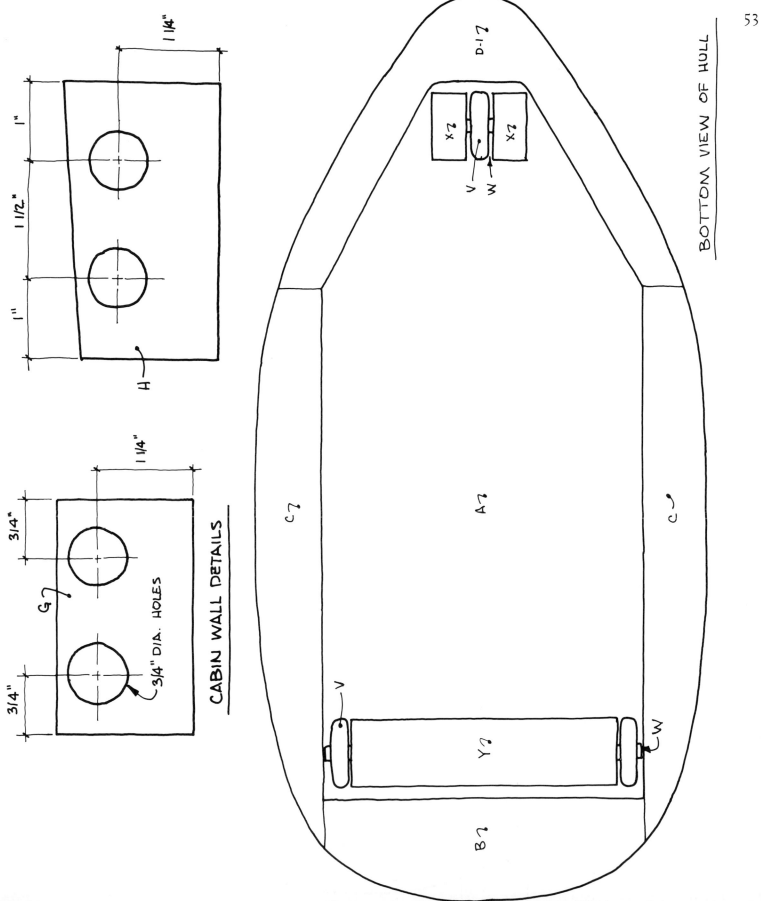

CABIN WALL DETAILS

3/4" DIA. HOLES

BOTTOM VIEW OF HULL

53

COMMUTER TRAIN

Moms and dads ride this kind of train to work every day so no wonder kids want to have one just like it. The trusty diesel engine and two passenger cars are designed to carry Little People for many miles of playful pleasure.

BEGIN CONSTRUCTION of the engine by cutting the bottoms (A), ends (B), wheel blocks (F), engine wheel block (L), and engine front parts (I–K) from ¾"-thick stock. Cut the engine sides (M) and ends (B) from ¼" stock.

Shopping List

Quantity	Description
3 feet	1 × 6 pine
3 feet	½" × 3" pine
8 feet	¼" × 5½" pine lattice
24	1" dia. × ¼" hardwood wheels
24	⁵⁄₃₂" dia. × ¹³⁄₁₆" axle pegs
1 foot	¼"-dia. hardwood dowel

Glue the engine front parts and engine wheel block together. When the glue has set, glue the engine sides, bottom, and end to this assembly. Use the engine side as a template and cut the rough shape of engine front with a band or coping saw. Finish the contouring with a sanding block and #120 grit sandpaper. Then drill a ⅞" hole in the engine front for the engineer.

Cut the roof (D) from ½"-thick stock and round the upper edges with a router or sanding block. Cut the ceiling (E), trim panels (N–O), and coupling (P) from ¼" stock.

Glue the trim panels to the sides of the engine and the ceiling to the un-derside of the roof. Check that the roof assembly fits snugly into the engines top.

Drill a ¼" hole in the coupling and glue in the coupling peg (Q), which is cut from ¼" dowel stock. Glue the wheel block and coupling to the bottom of the engine, then lay out and drill the ⁵⁄₃₂" axle holes in the wheel blocks. Place the wheels on the axles and glue the axles to the wheel blocks.

Construction of the cars is the same as the engine. Lay out and drill five 1¼" holes in the sides for windows and ⅞" holes in the bottom to hold the passengers.

Assemble the car sides, bottom, and

ends with glue. Glue the ceiling to the roof and check the fit in the car's top. Glue the wheel blocks and one coupling with a coupling peg to the bottom of the car. Glue a coupling block (R) between the bottom of the car and the other coupling to offset the coupling block. The last car needs only the offset coupling without the peg.

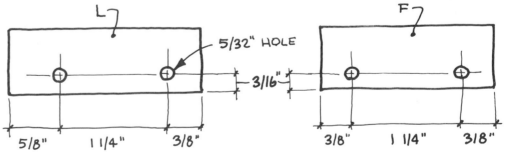

L

F

5/32" HOLE

3/16"

5/8" 1 1/4" 3/8"

3/8" 1 1/4" 3/8"

WHEEL BLOCKS

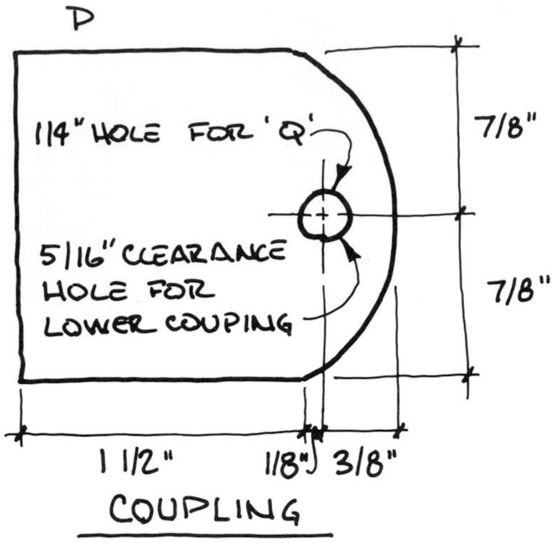
P
1/4" HOLE FOR 'Q'
5/16" CLEARANCE
HOLE FOR
LOWER COUPING
7/8"
7/8"
1 1/2"
1/8"
3/8"
COUPLING

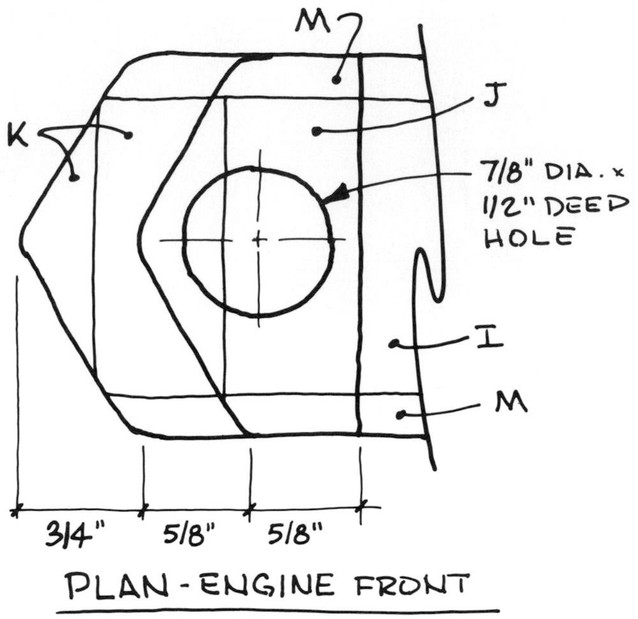
M
J
K
7/8" DIA. x
1/2" DEEP
HOLE
I
M
3/4"
5/8"
5/8"
PLAN - ENGINE FRONT

Parts List

Part	Name	No.	Size	Material
A	Bottoms	3	¾″ × 1¾″ × 8¾″	pine
B	Ends	5	¼″ × 1¾″ × 3¼″	pine
C	Sides	4	¼″ × 3¼″ × 9¼″	pine
D	Roofs	3	½″ × 2½″ × 9½″	pine
E	Ceilings	3	¼″ × 1¾″ × 8¾″	pine
F	Wheel blocks	5	¾″ × 1¾″ × 2″	pine
G	Wheels	24	1″ dia. × ¼″	hardwood wheel
H	Axles	24	5/32″ dia. × 13/16″	hardwood pin
I	Engine front	1	¾″ × 1¾″ × 3¼″	pine
J	Engine front	1	¾″ × 1¾″ × 1½″	pine
K	Engine fronts	2	¾″ × 1¾″ × 2¼″	pine
L	Engine wheel block	1	¾″ × 1¾″ × 2¼″	pine
M	Engine sides	2	¼″ × 4″ × 11¾″	pine
N	Trim panels	2	¼″ × 2″ × 4″	pine
O	Trim panels	2	¼″ × 2″ × 4″	pine
P	Couplings	4	¼″ × 1¾″ × 2″	pine
Q	Coupling pegs	2	¼″ dia. × ½″	pine
R	Coupling blocks	2	¼″ × 1¾″ × 1″	pine

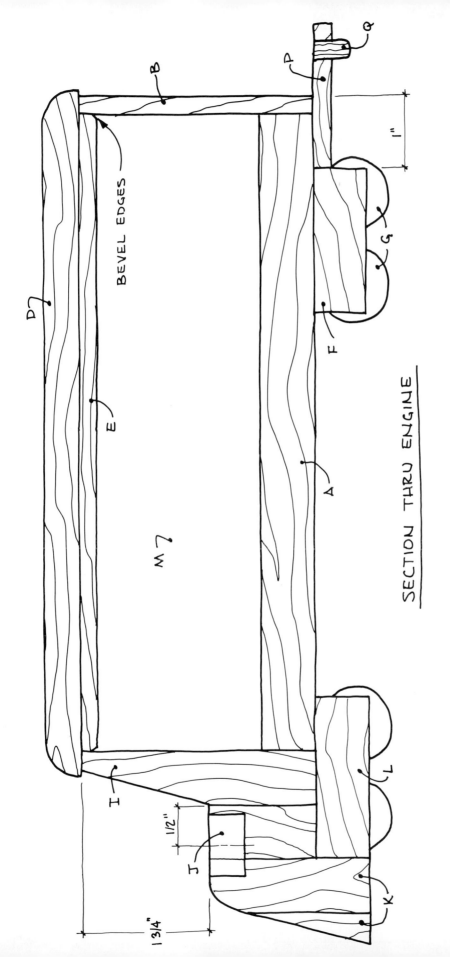

BEVEL EDGES

1"

1/2"

1 3/4"

SECTION THRU ENGINE

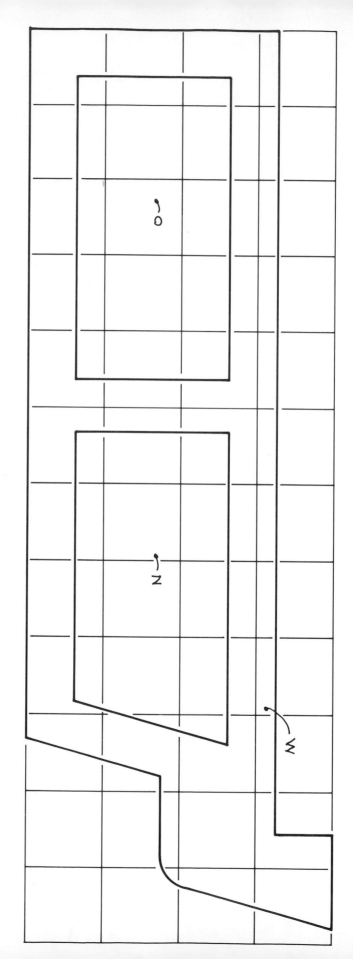

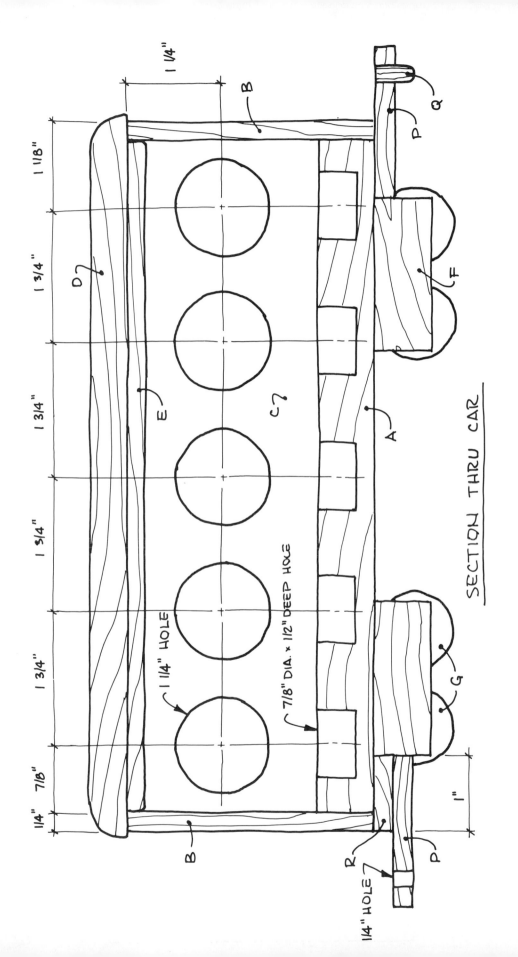

SECTION THRU CAR

1/4" 7/8"   1 3/4"   1 3/4"   1 3/4"   1 3/4"   1 3/4"   1 1/8"

1/4"

1 1/4" HOLE

7/8" DIA. × 1 1/2" DEEP HOLE

1/4" HOLE

1"

B

B

D

E

C

A

F

G

P

Q

R

P

AIR BUS

Last call for the people's express!
Build our air bus from standard pine
boards for your future pilot and you will
create a treasured toy. The pilot and
passengers drop into their seats from
overhead slots and peek through their own
windows. We designed our air bus to fit
plastic or wooden people you can purchase
or build from the pattern in our Introduction
(p. 9).

BEGIN CONSTRUCTION by enlarging all patterns. From these patterns transfer the body sides (B) to ¾"-thick pine and the body center (A), wing (C), and tail (D) to ½"-thick pine. To mark the location of the engine supports (F) on the tail and the window locations and rear axle holes on the

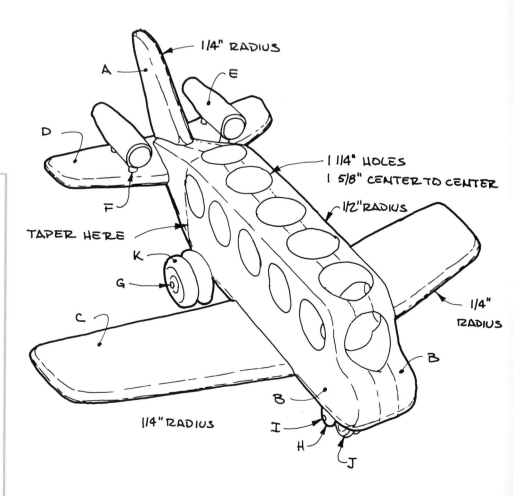

Shopping List

Quantity	Description
3 feet	½" × 5½" pine
3 feet	¾" × 5½" pine
1	3⁄16"-dia. birch dowel
1	¼"-dia. birch dowel
1	3⁄8"-dia. birch dowel
1	7⁄8"-dia. birch dowel
2	1"-dia. hardwood wheel
1	#3d finish nails (small box)

body sides punch through the patterns into the wood with a nail set.

Use a coping saw or jigsaw to cut the body parts to shape. Note that the body center is cut to final shape after assembly. This provides a flat entry for the drill when making the windshield in the front of the plane. Cut the wing and tail parts to shape.

Carefully align the wing and tail slots, then glue the body parts together. Drill the door holes in the top of the body first. The passenger compartments are formed with two holes. Make the 1¼″ holes first, then drill in the ⅞″ hole. The windows are made by drilling 1¼″

holes partially through the side of the body. Finish the hole from the other side. Begin the hole for the windshield in the square front section of the body center and carefully drill into the flight deck.

Lay out and drill two ⅜″ holes for the front wheel struts (H) in the underside of the body. Drill a ⁹⁄₃₂″ hole for the main landing gear on the body side. Check to see there is clearance for the axle to turn freely. After all holes are machined in the body, cut the center body (A) to match the body sides in front and along the top.

Sand or plane the body sides to a

smooth taper near the tail area according to the plan. Sand all parts with #120 grit abrasive paper. Round over the edges of the tail and wings with a sanding block or router with ¼″ round-over bit. Radius the body sides with a ½″ roundover bit or sand by hand. Smooth the inside of the passenger compartments with abrasive paper wrapped around a dowel.

Cut the engines (E) from ⅞″-dia. dowel stock. Drill two ¼″-dia. holes in each for the engine supports (F). Taper the rear of the engines and sand smooth. Cut the engine supports and assemble the tail and engines with glue. Then

62

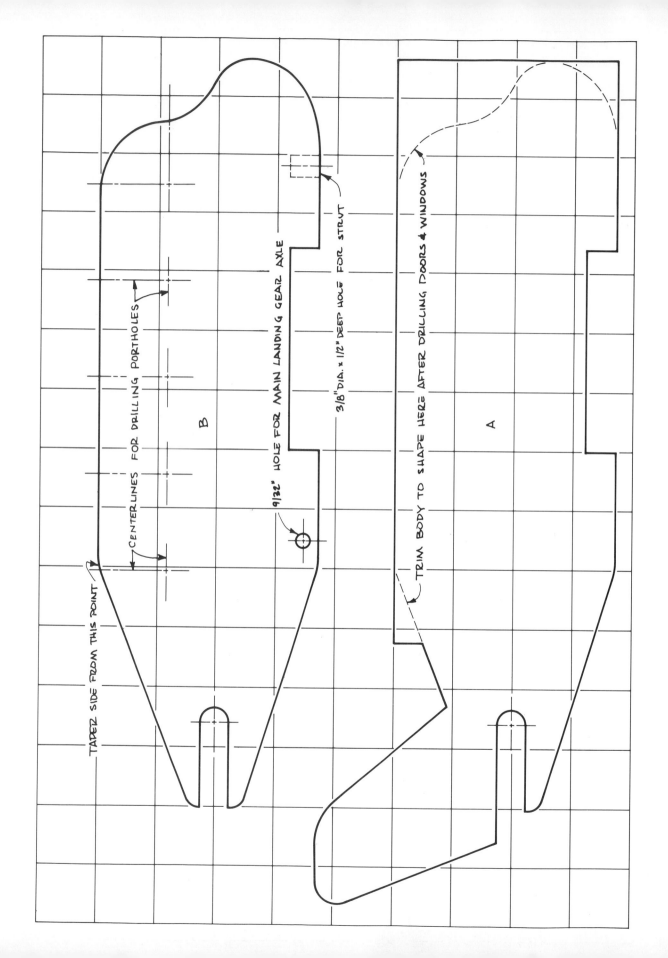

TAPER SIDE FROM THIS POINT

CENTERLINES FOR DRILLING PORTHOLES

B

9/32" HOLE FOR MAIN LANDING GEAR AXLE

3/8" DIA. x 1/2" DEEP HOLE FOR STRUT

TRIM BODY TO SHAPE HERE AFTER DRILLING DOORS & WINDOWS

A

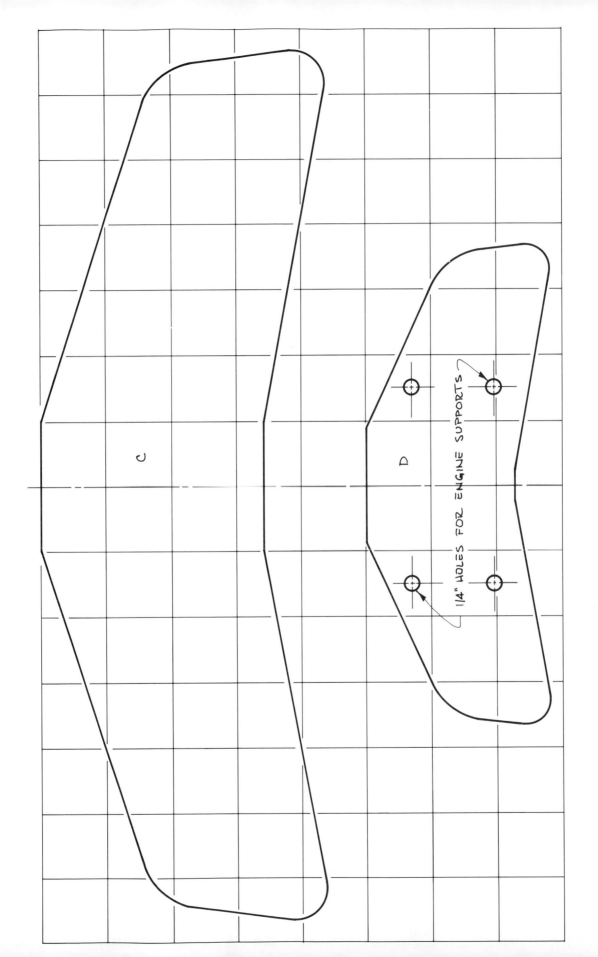

C

D

1/4" HOLES FOR ENGINE SUPPORTS

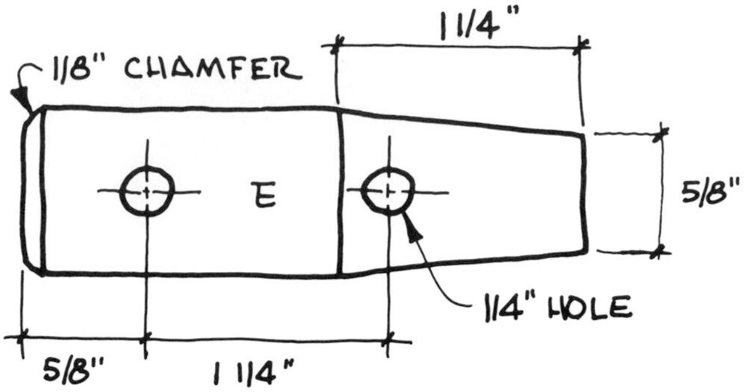
1/8" CHAMFER
1 1/4"
E
5/8"
1/4" HOLE
5/8"
1 1/4"

ENGINE DETAIL

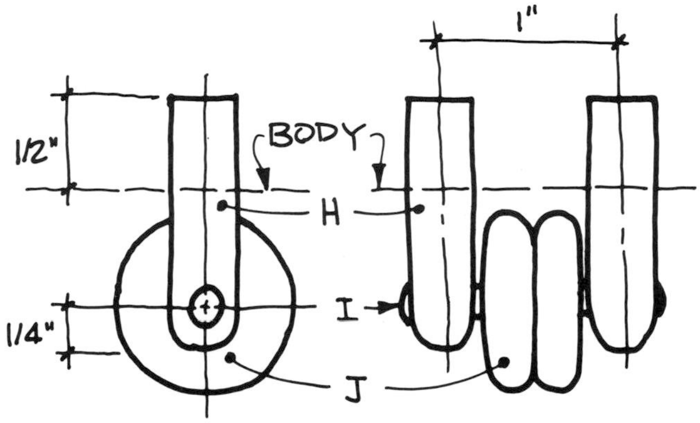
1"
1/2"
BODY
H
I
1/4"
J

STRUT DETAIL

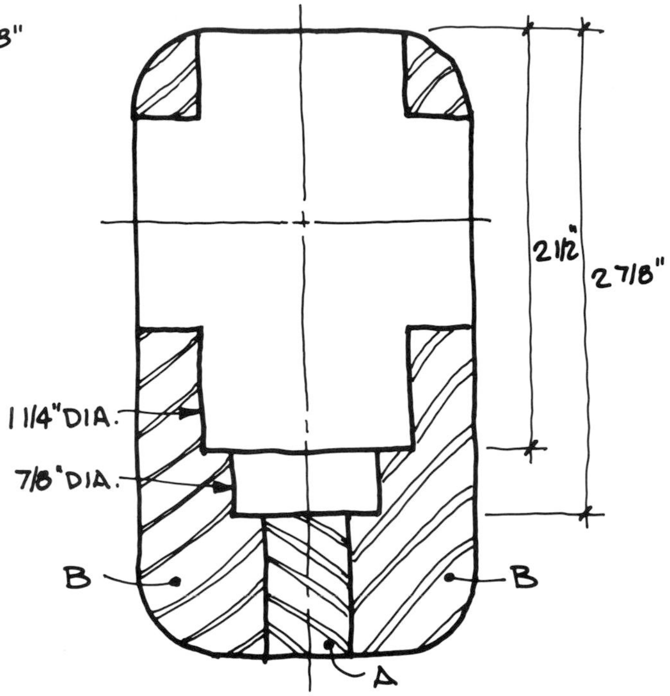
1 1/4"DIA.
7/8"DIA.
B
B
A
2 1/2"
2 7/8"

SECTION THRU BODY

glue the tail assembly in place. Attach the wings to the body with glue and #3d finish nails.

Make the struts (H) for the front wheel from ⅜″ dowel stock. Drill the 3⁄16″ hole for the front axle (I) first, then cut to length. Enlarge the front wheel holes for easy turning. Assemble the struts, axle, and wheels and glue in place.

Glue two wheels (K) to the rear axle (G), insert the axle into the plane body rear axle hole and check for free movement. Then glue on the other set of wheels.

We used plastic toy people for our pilot and passengers. If you want to make your own, enlarge the people pattern on page 10 and use it as a guide when turning your own from 1″ dowel stock.

Apply a clear wipe-on finish to the air bus, and its crew is ready to take off.

Parts List

Part	Name	No.	Size	Material
A	Body center	1	cut from pattern	½″ pine
B	Body sides	2	cut from pattern	¾″ pine
C	Wing	1	cut from pattern	½″ pine
D	Tail	1	cut from pattern	½″ pine
E	Engines	2	⅞″ dia. × 2⅞″	⅞″ birch dowel
F	Engine supports	4	¼″ dia. × ¾″	¼″ birch dowel
G	Rear axle	1	¼″ dia. × 4⅛″	¼″ birch dowel
H	Struts	2	⅜″ dia. × 1⅜″	⅜″ birch dowel
I	Front axle	1	3⁄16″ dia. × 1½″	3⁄16″ birch dowel
J	Front wheels	2	1″ dia. × ¼″	1″ hardwood wheel
K	Rear wheels	4	1½″ dia. × ½″	1½″ hardwood

TRACTOR

Little ones will love playing farmer with this pine tractor. They can hitch it to a flatbed trailer and install the removable partitioned side panels. Your small farmhand will enjoy hours of playful fun loading and unloading his goods with this sturdy little workhorse.

Shopping List

Quantity	Description
1 foot	2 × 4 pine
1 foot	1 × 4 pine
2 feet	½″ × 6″ pine
2 feet	¼″ × 3½″ pine lattice
1 foot	¼″-dia. hardwood dowel
1 foot	⅜″-dia. hardwood dowel
1 foot	³⁄₁₆″-dia. hardwood dowel
1 foot	1″-dia. hardwood dowel
6	1″ dia. × ¼″ hardwood wheels

BEGIN CONSTRUCTION by making the engine (B) from 1½″ pine stock. Cut the frame (A), step (F), and seat (G) from ½″ stock. Then cut the cab front (C), cab sides (D), and roof (E) from ¼″ lattice stock.

Bevel the top and front of the engine, then make a matching bevel on the front corners of the frame. Lay out and drill ¼″ holes for the radiator cap (J) and exhaust pipe (K) in the engine. Drill a ⅜″ hole in the underside of the frame for the strut (L) and a ¼″ hole in the rear of the frame for the hitch (Q). Drill a ⅞″ hole in the seat for the farmer.

Lay out the shape of the windows on the cab sides, then drill ¼″ holes in the corners to form the radius. Cut the window out with a coping saw. Sand all parts smooth with #120 grit sandpaper.

Glue the engine, cab front, step, and seat to the frame. Lay out and drill the ¼″ hole for the steering column (I) in the cab front. Cut the steering wheel (H) from 1″ dowel stock and glue it to the steering column. Glue this assembly to the cab front, checking that your farmer will fit into his seat behind the wheel. Assemble the cab parts and glue them to the frame.

Cut the strut from ⅜″ dowel stock and drill a ⁷⁄₃₂″ hole for the axle (M). Glue the strut into the hole in the underside of the frame, checking that the axle hole is aligned properly.

Make the axle from ³⁄₁₆″ dowel stock and glue one end into a small wheel

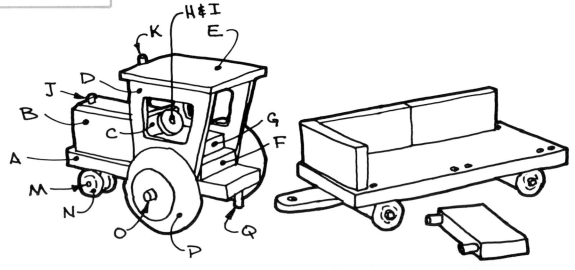

(N). When the glue has set, insert the wheel and axle into the strut and glue on the other wheel.

Drill the ⁷⁄₁₆″ axle hole through the frame. Insert the axle (O) and glue on the large wheels (P). Glue the hitch (Q) into its hole, add the radiator cap (J) and exhaust pipe (K), and your tractor is ready to haul away.

The trailer is easy to make. Cut the trailer bed (R) and side panels (S) from ½″ stock. Make the wheel blocks (U) from ¾″ stock and the tongue (W) from ¼″ lattice stock.

Lay out and drill the ⁵⁄₁₆″ holes for the pegs (T) in the trailer bed and side panels, then glue the pegs into the side panels. Drill a ⁵⁄₁₆″ hole in the tongue for the hitch and glue it and the wheel blocks to the bottom of the trailer bed.

Attach the wheels to the trailer by drilling ⁵⁄₃₂″ holes for the axle pegs (V) in the ends of the wheel blocks. Put a small amount of glue in these holes and insert the axles and wheels.

Apply a natural finish to both tractor and trailer. Load it with Little People that you can make yourself (see p. 10) and fill the trailer with marbles or candy corn.

Parts List

Part	Name	No.	Size	Material
A	Frame	1	½″ × 2″ × 7½″	pine
B	Engine	1	1½″ × 1¾″ × 3½″	pine
C	Cab front	1	¼″ × 1½″ × 2″	pine
D	Cab sides	2	¼″ × 3½″ × 4″	pine
E	Roof	1	¼″ × 3″ × 4″	pine
F	Stop	1	½″ × 2″ × 2½″	pine
G	Seat	1	½″ × 2″ × 2″	pine
H	Steering wheel	1	1″ dia. × ³⁄₁₆″	hardwood dowel
I	Steering column	1	¼″ dia. × 1″	hardwood dowel
J	Radiator cap	1	¼″ dia. × ½″	hardwood dowel
K	Exhaust pipe	1	¼″ dia. × 2¾″	hardwood dowel
L	Strut	1	⅜″ dia. × 2″	hardwood dowel
M	Axle	1	³⁄₁₆″ dia. × 1″	hardwood dowel
N	Wheels	6	1″ dia. × ¼″	hardwood wheel
O	Axle	1	⅜″ dia. × 5⅜″	hardwood dowel
P	Wheels	2	3″ dia. × 1⅛″	hardwood wheel
Q	Hitch	1	¼″ dia. × ⅞″	hardwood dowel
R	Trailer bed	1	½″ × 4″ × 8¾″	pine
S	Side panels	6	½″ × 1½″ × 3¾″	pine
T	Pegs	12	¼″ dia. × 1″	hardwood dowel
U	Wheel blocks	2	¾″ × ⅞″ × 3″	pine
V	Axle pegs	4	⁵⁄₃₂″ dia. × ¹³⁄₁₆″	axle peg
W	Tongue	1	¼″ × 1″ × 2¾″	pine

68

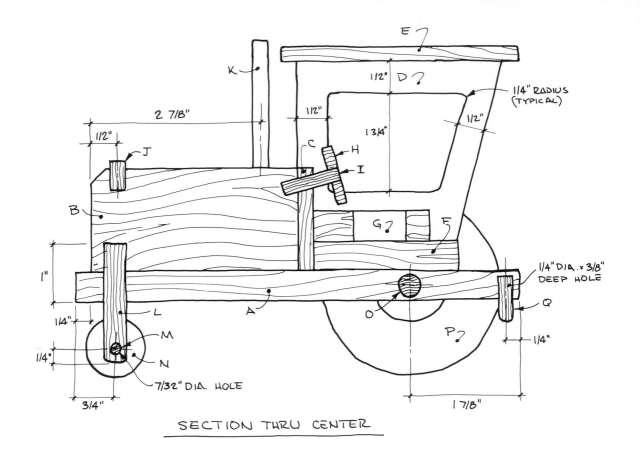

SECTION THRU CENTER

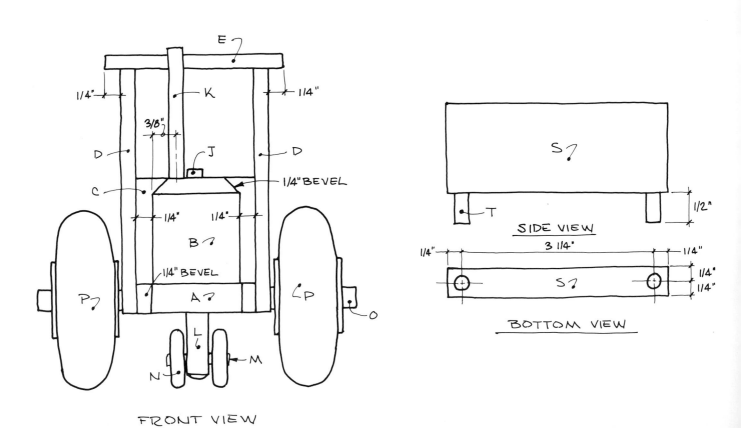

FRONT VIEW

SIDE VIEW

BOTTOM VIEW

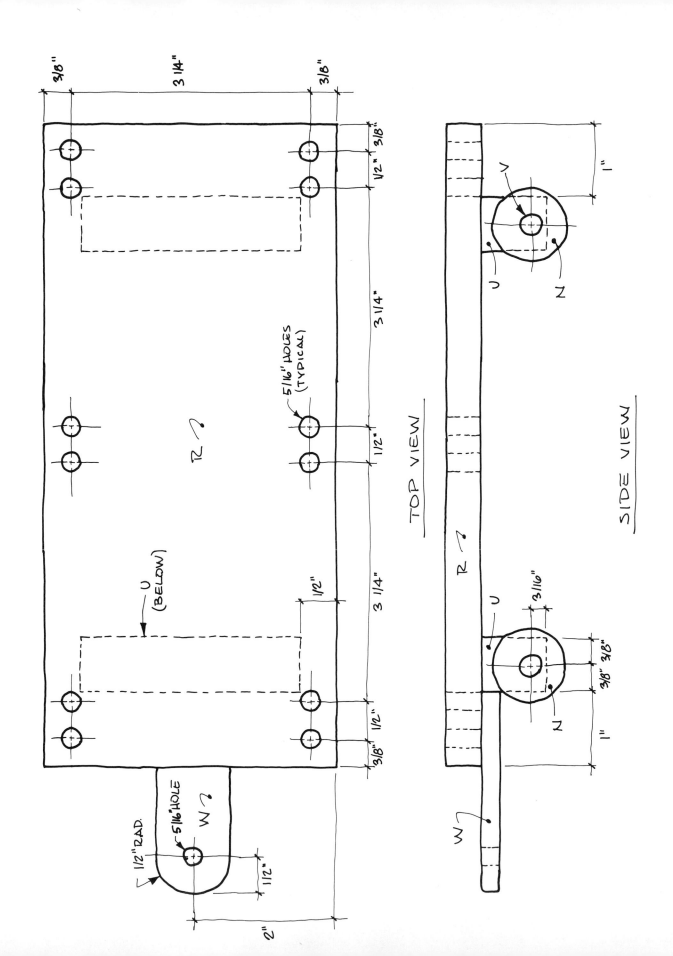

TOP VIEW

SIDE VIEW

3/8"

3 1/4"

3/8"

3/8"

1/2"

3/8"

3 1/4"

1/2"

3 1/4"

1/2"

3/8"

1/2"

3/8"

5/16" HOLES
(TYPICAL)

R

U
(BELOW)

1/2" RAD.

5/16" HOLE

1/2"

2"

V

N

1"

U

R

W

3/16"

3/8" 3/8"

1"

U

N

W

DEXTER THE DRAGON

Guaranteed to put a smile on any child's face, this whimsical dragon is an easy-to-build project made of simple pine. Dexter's backbone is made of felt and his segmented body is easily glued together.

Shopping List

Quantity	Description
1 foot	1 × 6 pine
1 foot	½″ × 4″ pine
1 foot	¼″ × 1½″ pine lattice
4	2″-dia. axle pegs
⅓ yard	green felt
scrap	red felt

BEGIN CONSTRUCTION by enlarging the patterns for Dexter's body, head, and tail parts. Transfer the shape of Dexter's body halves (A) and the location of the axles to ¾″-thick stock. Drill ⁷⁄₃₂″-dia. holes through these axle layout marks.

Lay out his head halves (B) on ¾″-thick stock. Copy the three neck (F–H) and tail (C–E) segments on ½″ stock. Trace the tail (I) and mouth (J) segments on ¼″ stock and then cut all parts to size.

Use a band saw, belt, or disk sander to bevel the top and bottom edges of the body parts 15 degrees. Bevel the connecting edges of the segments 30 degrees. The size of these bevels is not critical, just make them all the same.

Sand the segments smooth with #120 grit sandpaper. Apply a wipe-on oil finish to the exposed sides of these parts before you glue them to the felt backbone. Apply finish to the wheels and the head of the axle.

Trace the shape of the backbone on green felt. Cut the felt slightly oversize along the bottom and around the head

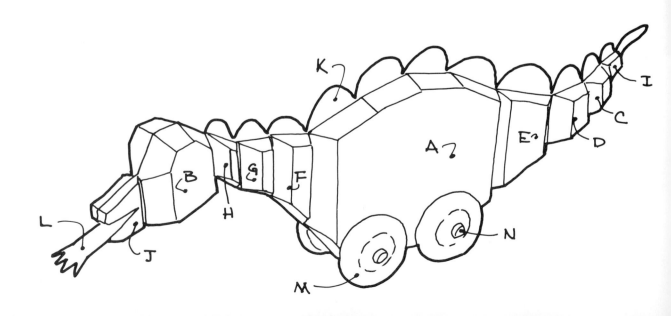

so you can trim it flush with a razor after the body segments are glued in place.

Apply glue to the back of the body segments, keeping the glue away from the outer edges. Assemble Dexter beginning with the body. Apply the seg-ments, aligning them with the top of the felt so each segment has its own hump. Work on one side and then turn Dexter over and glue on the other seg-ments. Place a small amount of glue in the bottom of his mouth and insert the felt fire (L).

Place the wheels on the axle pegs and apply a small amount of glue to the axle holes. Insert the pegs so the wheels are held close to the body but move freely. Dexter is now ready to scoot about with his head swaying and his tail wagging.

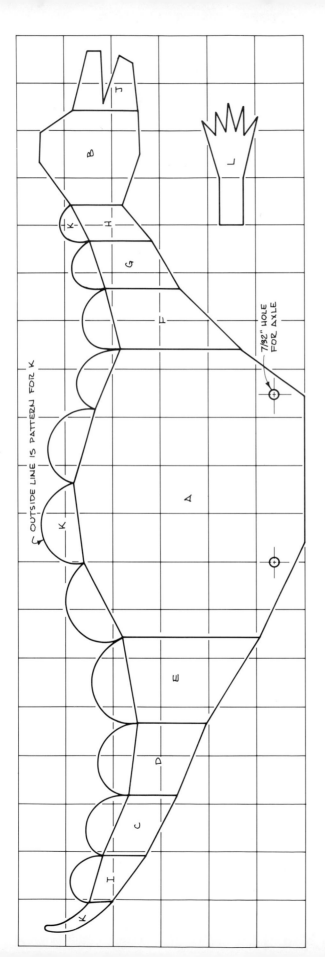

OUTSIDE LINE IS PATTERN FOR K

7/32" HOLE FOR AXLE

Parts List

Part	Name	No.	Size	Material
A	Body halves	2	cut from pattern	3/4" pine
B	Head halves	2	cut from pattern	3/4" pine
C	Tail segments	2	cut from pattern	1/2" pine
D	Tail segments	2	cut from pattern	1/2" pine
E	Tail segments	2	cut from pattern	1/2" pine
F	Neck segments	2	cut from pattern	1/2" pine
G	Neck segments	2	cut from pattern	1/2" pine
H	Neck segments	2	cut from pattern	1/2" pine
I	Tail segments	2	cut from pattern	1/4" pine
J	Mouth segments	2	cut from pattern	1/4" pine
K	Felt backbones	2	cut from pattern	green felt
L	Felt fire	2	cut from pattern	red felt
M	Wheels	4	2" dia.	hardwood wheel
N	Axles	4	7/32" × 1 1/4"	axle peg

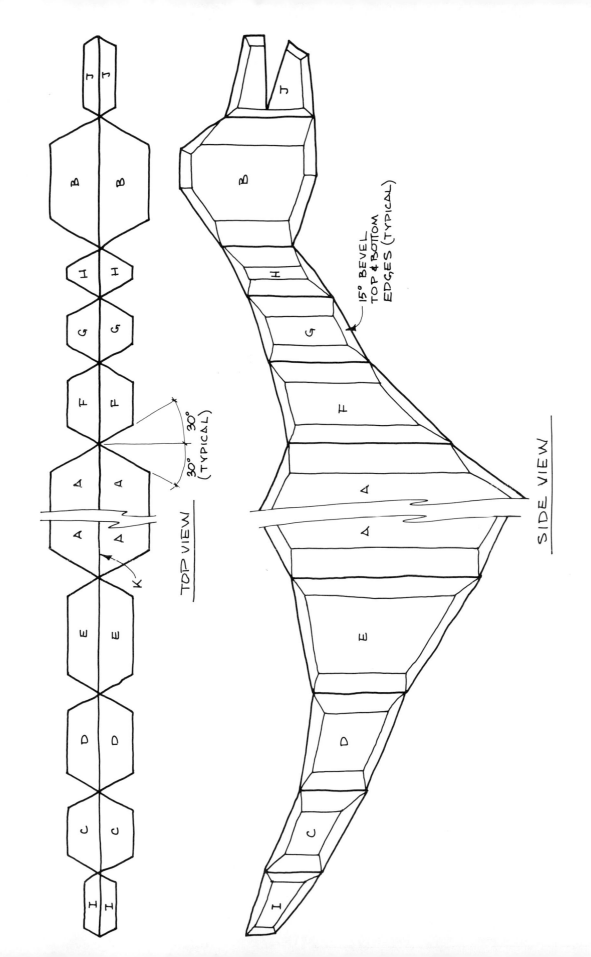

TOP VIEW

30° 30°
30°
(TYPICAL)

K

SIDE VIEW

15° BEVEL
TOP & BOTTOM
EDGES (TYPICAL)

73

PETE THE PENGUIN

Here's a perky penguin named Pete, a new and novel pull toy. Perched on his own iceberg Pete is ready to be pulled and played with. His paddlelike wings flip up and down as he moves along his way.

BEGIN CONSTRUCTION by enlarging the patterns for the head (A), front body filler (B), rear body filler (C), shoulders (D), sides (E), wings (F), and feet (G). Transfer the patterns for the head and body fillers to ¾″ birch and the other parts to ½″ walnut. Cut the shoulders and sides from the same piece of walnut so the grain matches.

Shopping List

Quantity	Description
2 feet	⁵⁄₄″ × 6″ birch
3 feet	¾″ × 2″ birch
1 foot	½″ × 8″ birch
3 feet	½″ × 6″ walnut
1 foot	¼″-dia. hardwood dowel
6	2″-dia. hardwood wheel
2	⁷⁄₃₂″-dia. axle peg
2 feet	12-gauge wire
2	plastic eyes
2	⅝″ × 1½″ steel angle brackets
4	1½″-long #6 FH wood screw
4	¾″-long #6 FH wood screw
4	½″-long #6 FH wood screw

Notch the sides according to the plan. Bevel the inside edge of these notches with sandpaper or a chisel to provide clearance for the wing brackets. Glue the sides to the front and rear body fillers, then place the head in position and glue the shoulders to it. Check the alignment of all body parts. Then remove the head and shoulders before the glue dries.

Cut the side aprons (I), ends (J), and corners (K) from ¾″ birch and the base (H) from ½″ birch stock. Glue up the iceberg base according to the plan. Fill all open joints with wood filler, sand the sides smooth, then paint the iceberg base white.

Cut the opening on the base for the drive wires and notch the underside of the sides for the axle (O) according to the plan. Make the wheel blocks (L) from ¾″ stock, then mark and drill the ⁷⁄₃₂″ holes for the axle pegs (P). Insert an axle peg into the wheel (M) and glue the peg to the wheel block. Glue the wheel blocks to the underside of the iceberg.

Make the drive-wheel assembly next. On one wheel mark the location of the crank (N). Drill a ¼″ hole in a piece of scrap and insert a short section of dowel in the hole. Stack the four drive wheels on the dowel and drill the ¼″ crank hole through all the wheels at the same time.

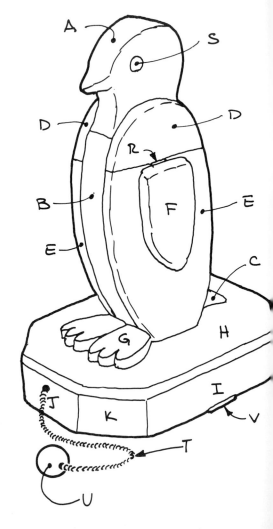

Glue the wheels to the crank and axle according to the plan. When the glue is dry, cut the axle away between the center two drive wheels. Drill a small hole through the wheels into the axle and crank and drive a wire brad into it to lock the wheels in place.

Make the wing brackets (R) from steel angles. Use a hacksaw to cut the brackets then bend them according to the plan. Attach the wing brackets to the back of the wing with ½" screws. Note that the brackets should be positioned so that when they are in the bracket slot the bent flanges face one another. Check that these brackets clear and have sufficient movement.

Mount the body assembly to the iceberg with four 1½" screws. Place the drive-axle assembly in the notches in the bottom of the iceberg. Secure the axle with the axle blocks (V) and four ¾" screws. Then check for free movement of the wheels.

Bend the drive wires (Q) to shape, then hook one end through the hole in the wing bracket. Hook the other end over the crank. Turn the drive wheels and check the wing movement. If needed, adjust the length of the drive wires for best action.

Glue the head assembly to the body and sand smooth with #120 grit sandpaper. Glue the feet in place, then apply an oil finish. Mark and drill the hole for the eyes (S) and glue them in place.

Drill a small hole in the front of the iceberg and attach the pull cord (T) and handle (U). Pete is now ready to flap his wings and chase after any small-fry who pulls him across the floor.

Parts List

Part	Name	No.	Size	Material
A	Head	1	cut from pattern	⁵⁄₄" birch
B	Front body filler	1	cut from pattern	⁵⁄₄" birch
C	Rear body filler	1	cut from pattern	⁵⁄₄" birch
D	Shoulders	2	cut from pattern	½" walnut
E	Sides	2	cut from pattern	½" walnut
F	Wings	2	cut from pattern	½" walnut
G	Feet	2	cut from pattern	½" walnut
H	Base	1	½" × 7" × 10"	birch
I	Side aprons	2	¾" × 1½" × 6"	birch
J	Ends	2	¾" × 1½" × 3"	birch
K	Corners	4	¾" × 1½" × 2¹³⁄₁₆"	birch
L	Wheel blocks	2	¾" × 1½" × 1¾"	birch
M	Wheels	6	2" dia. × ⁵⁄₈"	hardwood wheel
N	Crank	1	¼" dia. × 5"	hardwood dowel
O	Axle	1	¼" dia. × 6¼"	hardwood dowel
P	Axle pegs	2	⁷⁄₃₂" × 1¼"	hardwood dowel
Q	Drive wires	2	12" long	12-gauge wire
R	Wing brackets	2	⁵⁄₈" × 1½"	steel angle
S	Eyes	2	⁵⁄₈" dia.	plastic eye
T	Pull cord	1	⅛" dia. × 30"	cord
U	Handle	1	1½" dia.	hardwood ball
V	Axle blocks	2	¼" × ½" × 1¾"	birch

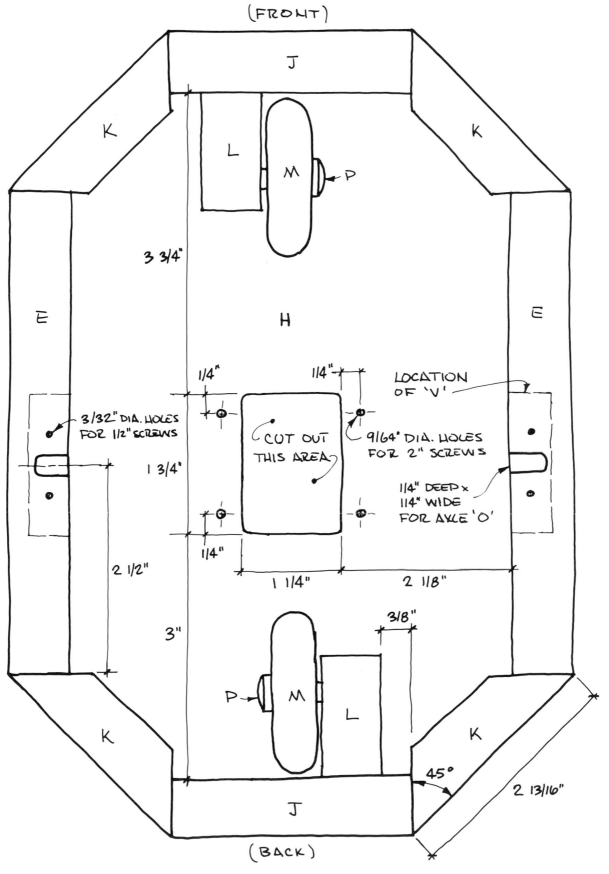

BOTTOM VIEW OF BASE

78

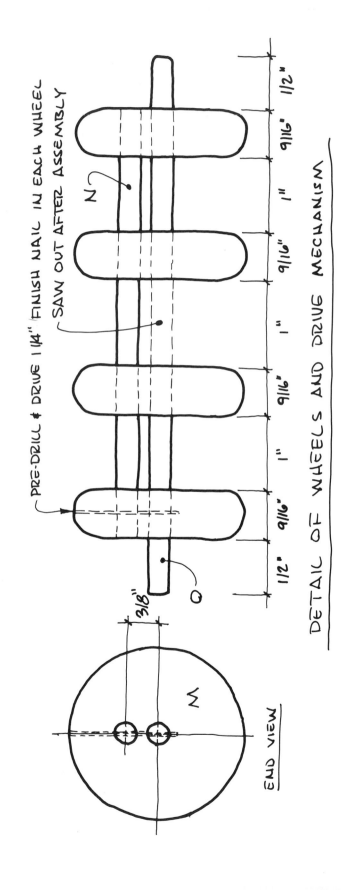

PRE-DRILL & DRIVE 1 1/4" FINISH NAIL IN EACH WHEEL

SAW OUT AFTER ASSEMBLY

N

O

1/2"   9/16"   1"   9/16"   1"   9/16"   1"   9/16"   1/2"

DETAIL OF WHEELS AND DRIVE MECHANISM

3/8"

W

END VIEW

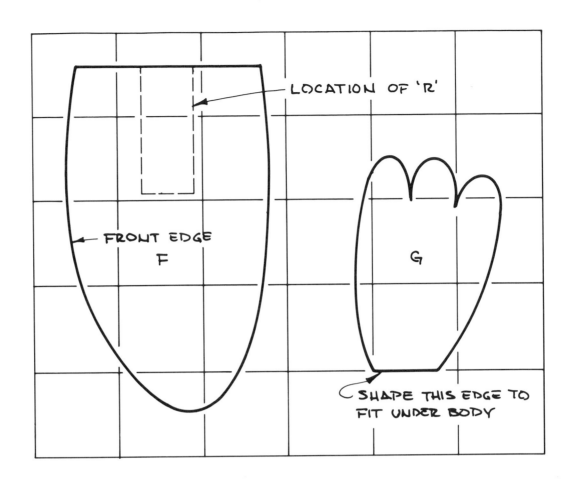

LOCATION OF 'R'

FRONT EDGE
F

G

SHAPE THIS EDGE TO
FIT UNDER BODY

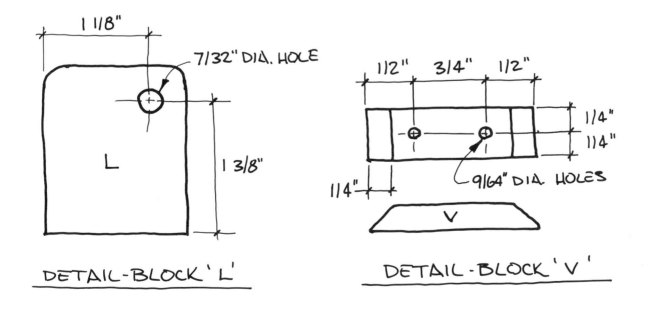

1 1/8"

7/32" DIA. HOLE

L

1 3/8"

DETAIL-BLOCK 'L'

1/2"   3/4"   1/2"

1/4"

1/4"

1/4"

9/64" DIA HOLES

V

DETAIL-BLOCK 'V'

80

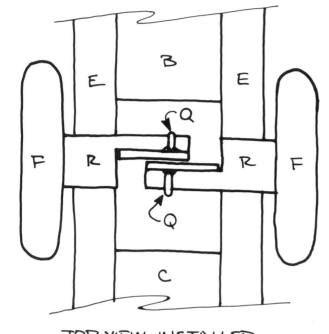

TOP VIEW INSTALLED
(PARTS 'A' & 'D' REMOVED)

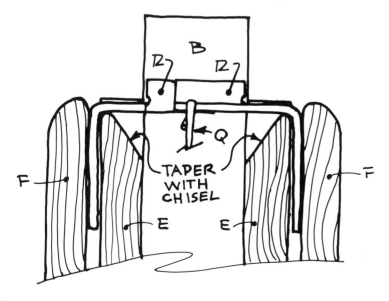

SECTION LOOKING FORWARD
(PARTS 'A' & 'D' REMOVED)

TAPER WITH CHISEL

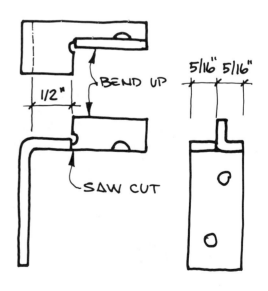

BEND UP

1/2"

SAW CUT

5/16" 5/16"

BRACKET BENDING DETAIL

BRACKET DETAILS

MOTHER DUCK AND BABY DUCK

With flapping rubber feet and a jaunty smile, Mother Duck and her little duckling will become your child's favored push toy. A dowel handle directs the winsome twosome that waddles on easy-to-make wheels with adorable flapping feet.

Shopping List

Quantity	Description
2 feet	1 × 12 pine
1 foot	½" × 8" pine
3 feet	¼" × 5½" pine lattice
1 foot	⅝"-dia. hardwood dowel
1 foot	½"-dia. hardwood dowel
3 feet	⅜" hardwood dowel
1 foot	¼" hardwood dowel
1	1½" wood ball
small box	¾" wire brads
scrap	innertube rubber
2	½" Velcro pads (hook side)
1 foot	½" Velcro strap

BEGIN CONSTRUCTION by enlarging the pattern for the mother and baby duck. Transfer the shape and cut out the mother's body (A) and wheels (D) from ¾" stock. Transfer and cut the shape of the body (K), bill (C), and wheels (N) from ½" stock. Lay out and cut the bill (M) and wings (B) and (L) from ¼" stock. Sand all parts with #120 grit sandpaper, rounding the sharp edges.

Assemble Mother Duck first. Glue on the wings, using several ¾" wire brads to hold them in position while the glue dries. Mark the location, then drill the ⅝" hole for the axle housing

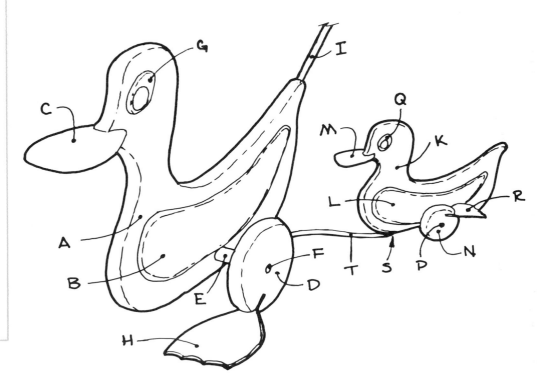

Parts List—**MOTHER DUCK**

Part	Name	No.	Size	Material
A	Body	1	cut from pattern	¾″ pine
B	Wings	2	cut from pattern	¼″ pine
C	Bill	1	cut from pattern	½″ pine
D	Wheels	2	cut from pattern	¾″ pine
E	Axle housing	1	⅝″ dia. × 4″	birch dowel
F	Axle shaft	1	⅜″ dia. × 5⅝″	birch dowel
G	Eyes	2	cut from pattern	¼″ pine
H	Feet	2	cut from pattern	innertube rubber
I	Push stick	1	⅜″ dia. × 24″	birch dowel
J	Handle ball	1	1½″ dia.	ball

Parts List—**BABY DUCK**

Part	Name	No.	Size	Material
K	Body	1	cut from pattern	½″ pine
L	Wings	2	cut from pattern	¼″ pine
M	Bill	1	cut from pattern	¼″ pine
N	Wheels	2	cut from pattern	½″ pine
O	Axle housing	1	½″ dia. × 2¼″	birch dowel
P	Axle shaft	1	¼″ dia. × 3⅜″	birch dowel
Q	Eyes	2	cut from pattern	¼″ pine
R	Feet	2	cut from pattern	innertube rubber
S	Hooks	2	½″ dia	Velcro (hook side)
T	Pull strap	1	½″ × 8″	Velcro strap

(E). Drill a ⅜″ hole for the push stick (I) in the tail of your duck. Cut the push stick from dowel stock and glue one end into a ⅜″ hole in the handle ball (J). Slip-fit the other end into the duck body.

Install the bill by sanding its end until it fits into the slot. When you are satisfied with the fit, glue the bill in place.

Make the axle assembly by drilling a ⅜″ hole in the center of the axle housing. If you don't have a long drill cut the axle in half and drill both parts separately. If you drilled the axle housing in one piece then glue it into the body with 1⅝″ projecting from each side. Otherwise insert the axle shaft (F) into the axle housing to keep both parts in alignment in the duck's body. Move the axle shaft several times while the glue sets to be certain it is not stuck to the axle housings inside.

Clamp the wheels together and sand their edges smoothly to make a matched pair. Cut the slot for the floppy feet (H) and drill the axle hole while they are together. Glue the wheels to the ends of the axle shaft and check that they do not wobble when turned.

Copy the shape of the eyes (G) on a scrap of wood and cut it to shape. Paint the eyeballs and allow them to dry. Then glue the eyes in place.

The Baby Duck is assembled in exactly the same way as its mother. (The axles are different diameter.) When both are completed, finish sand with #220 grit paper. We applied a clear easy-to-apply wipe-on finish. After the finish is dry install the floppy feet and the ducks are ready for a stroll.

84

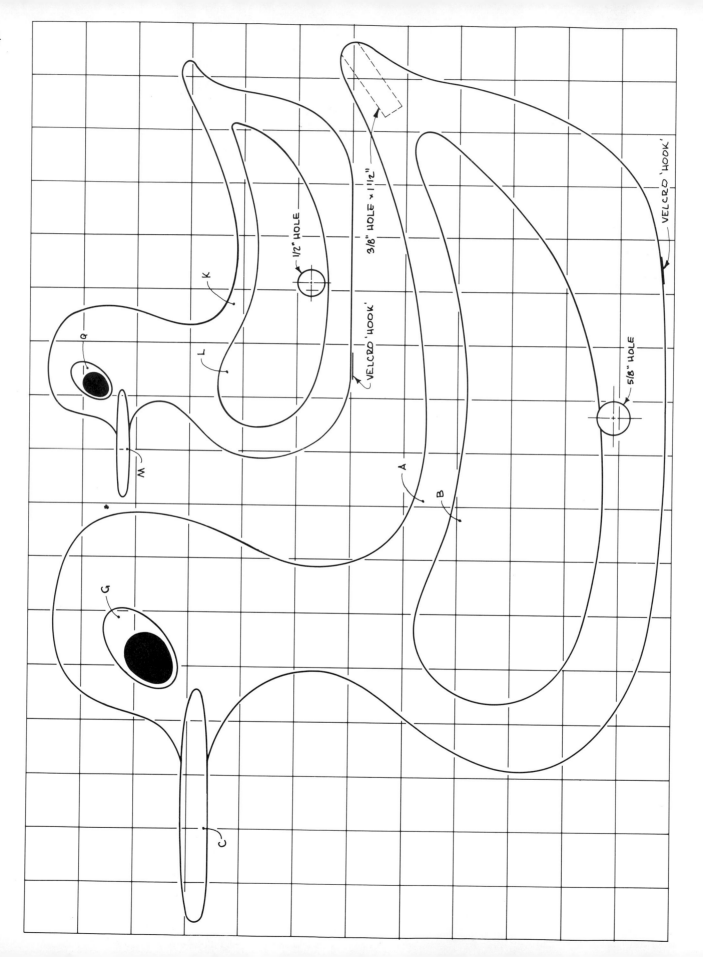

G

C

Q

W

K

L

1/2" HOLE

3/8" HOLE × 1¹/₂"

VELCRO 'HOOK'

VELCRO 'HOOK'

A

B

5/8" HOLE

VELCRO 'HOOK'

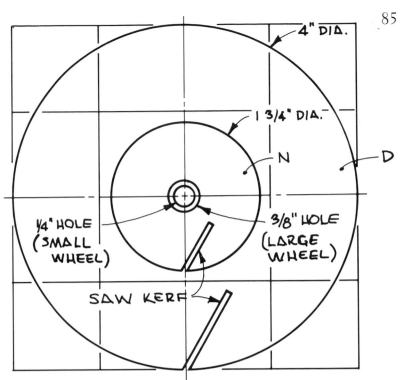

4" DIA.

1 3/4" DIA.

N

D

1/4" HOLE
(SMALL
WHEEL)

3/8" HOLE
(LARGE
WHEEL)

SAW KERF

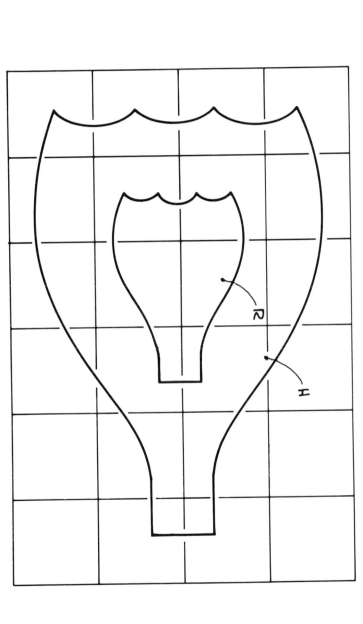

2

H

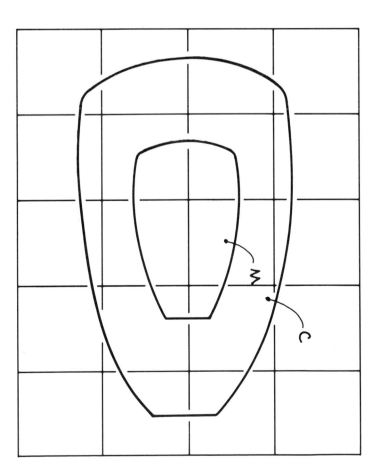

W

C

DOC'S HOUND

Made of walnut and birch, this hound dog is a low-slung, jaunty fellow. Always one to keep his nose to the ground, Doc's head bobs and his ears flop as you move him along.

Shopping List

Quantity	Description
1 foot	1 × 6 birch
1 foot	1 × 6 walnut
3 feet	½″ × 6″ walnut
2 feet	½″ × 4″ birch
1 foot	⅜″-dia. hardwood dowel
4	1½″-dia. wheels
4	⁷⁄₃₂″-dia. axle pegs
1	1″-long #6 screw
2	3″ rubber bands
6 inches	leather strip

BEGIN CONSTRUCTION by enlarging the patterns for the head (A), ears (B), sides (C), filler (D), and the front (E) and rear (F) legs. Transfer the head pattern to ¾″-thick birch and the legs to ½″ birch. Trace the ear and side patterns on ½″ walnut and the filler on ¾″-thick walnut stock. Use a coping or band saw to cut all parts to shape. Cut the head (J) and ear pivot (K) from ⅜″ hardwood dowel stock.

On the head, lay out then drill the ½″ eye holes and two ⁷⁄₁₆″ holes for the ear and head pivots. Mark the location, then drill the ⁷⁄₃₂″ holes for the axles (H) in the ends of the legs. Cut

two ¾″-long pieces of ½″ walnut dowel and glue them into the eye holes. Sand the eyes smooth after the glue has dried.

Clamp the sides together when drilling the ⅜″ head pivot hole to assure alignment. Drill a ⅜″ hole through the bottom of the filler for the rubber band. Use a router with a ⅜″ straight cutter or wood chisel to cut a shallow recess in the bottom of the filler, starting at the rubber band hole and extending toward the tail for 3 to 4 inches.

Glue the sides to the filler, then use a router and a ½″ roundover bit to radius all edges of the body. Also cut ¼″ radii on all edges of the ears, head, and

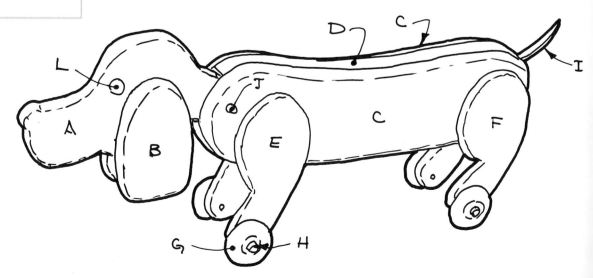

front and rear legs. Sand all edges smooth with #120 grit sandpaper, then follow with a final sanding using #220 grit paper.

Glue the front and rear legs to the body according to the plan. When the glue is dry, insert the axle pegs in the wheels and glue these pegs to the front and rear legs.

It is easier to finish the head and ears before they are assembled. We wiped on an oil finish and when dry, glued the ears to the ear pivot, checking that they move freely.

Pass a string through the rubber band hole and out through the head slot. Slip the rubber band through the hole in the end of the head and secure it by looping it over the end. Tie the end of the string to the rubber band. Pull the rubber band into the body with the string and align the head with the head pivot hole. Insert the head pivot dowel to hold the head in place. This dowel should fit tightly in the sides.

Pull the rubber band tight and loop it over the small screw in the end of the slot. Experiment with the amount of tension and the number of rubber bands needed to provide a bouncing action to Doc's head as he is pushed along.

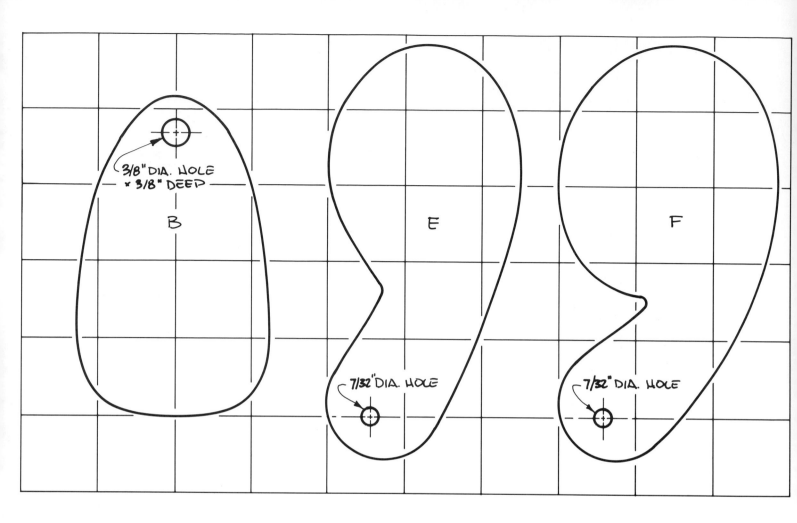

3/8" DIA. HOLE × 3/8" DEEP

B

E

F

7/32" DIA. HOLE

7/32" DIA. HOLE

Parts List

Part	Name	No.	Size	Material
A	Head	1	cut from pattern	¾" birch
B	Ears	2	cut from pattern	½" walnut
C	Sides	2	cut from pattern	½" walnut
D	Filler	1	cut from pattern	¾" walnut
E	Front legs	2	cut from pattern	½" birch
F	Rear legs	2	cut from pattern	½" birch
G	Wheels	4	1½" dia.	hardwood
H	Axles	4	7/32" dia. × 1¼"	hardwood peg
I	Tail	1	¼" × 2"	leather
J	Head pivot	1	⅜" dia. × 1¾"	hardwood dowel
K	Ear pivot	1	⅜" dia. × 1⅝"	hardwood dowel
L	Eyes	2	½" dia. × ¾"	walnut plug

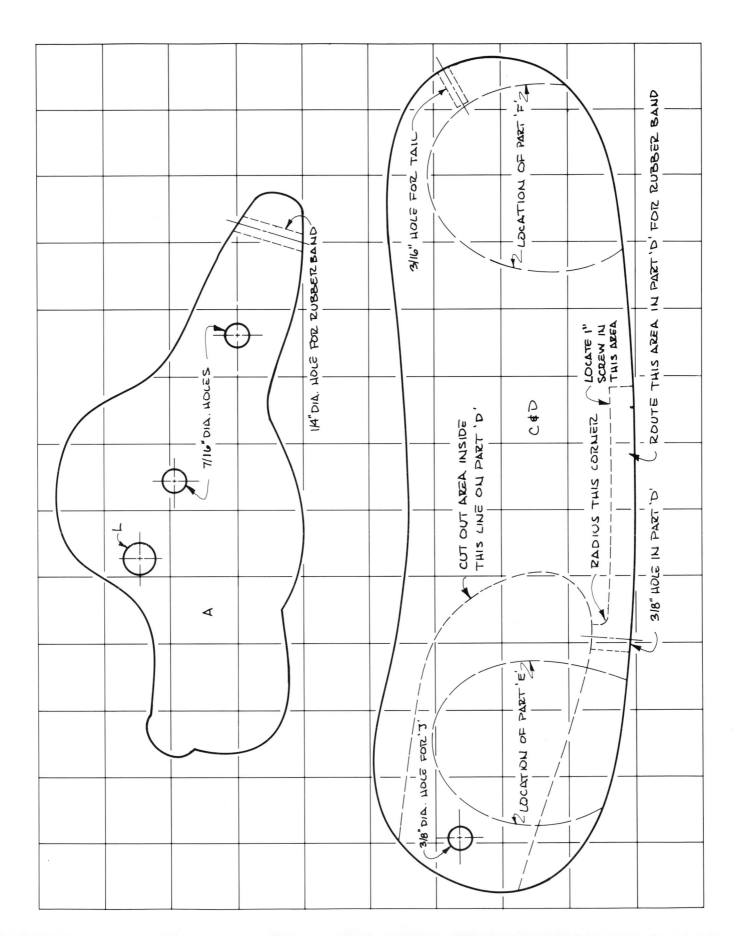

RASCAL RABBIT

This ingenious pull toy will become a special friend to any little boy or girl. Rascal is specially engineered to hippety-hop along the floor as a youngster pulls on his leash. His ears move too. When Rascal is sad his ears droop forward, and they can be flipped back when he's on the move.

BEGIN CONSTRUCTION by enlarging the patterns for the sides (A), body (B), rear legs (E), front legs (G), and ears (J). Transfer the pattern for the body to ¾″ birch stock and the others to ½″ stock. Then cut all parts to shape with a band or coping saw. Make the axle (D), rear leg pivot (F), and ear pivot (J) from ⅜″ hardwood dowel stock.

Cut a 4″-dia. circle from ½″ birch stock and mark location of the axle hole according to the plan. Note: This ⅜″ hole is placed ½″ off center to give Rascal his up-and-down hopping action. Glue the axle to the rear wheel.

Use a router and a ¼″ roundover bit to radius all edges of the ears, front and rear legs, sides, and the head and tail portion of the body. Stop all radii on the body where it contacts the sides.

Mark and drill the ½″ hole for the eyes and the ⁷⁄₁₆″ ear pivot (K) hole in the head portion of the body. Drill the

Shopping List	
Quantity	**Description**
2 feet	1″ × 8″ birch
5 feet	½″ × 8″ birch
1 foot	⅜″-dia. hardwood dowel
3 feet	heavy cord
2	1½″-dia. hardwood wheels
2	⁷⁄₃₂″-dia. axle pegs
2	⅜″ steel washers

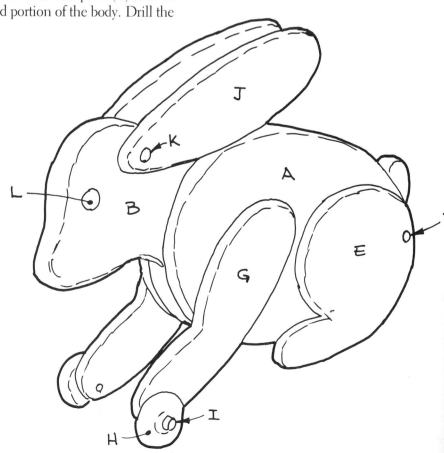

⁷⁄₁₆″ hole for the rear wheel axle through both sides at the same time to assure alignment. Check the fit of the axle; you might have to sand it slightly to get proper clearance. Mark and drill the ⁷⁄₃₂″ holes in the ends of the front legs for the axle pegs (I).

Glue the sides to the filler and place a metal washer on each side of the rear wheel axle when placing this assembly

in the axle holes. Glue walnut plugs into the eye holes. After the glue has dried, sand the eyes and all joints smooth.

Mark and drill the ⁷⁄₁₆″ hole for the rear leg pivot in the rear of the body assembly. Check that the pivot moves freely in the hole. Glue the front legs to the sides according to the plan. When the glue is dry, chip away glue squeeze-

out and give all parts a light sanding with #220 grit sandpaper.

We applied a wipe-on oil finish to all parts. When the finish is dry, glue the rear legs and ears to their pivot dowels. Insert the axle pegs into the wheels (H) and glue these pegs to the front legs. Make sure the wheels turn freely.

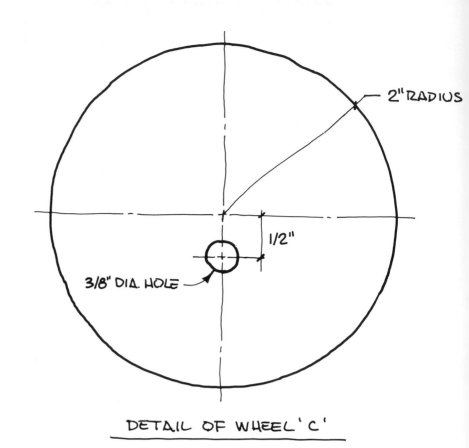

2" RADIUS

1/2"

3/8" DIA. HOLE

DETAIL OF WHEEL 'C'

Parts List

Part	Name	No.	Size	Material
A	Sides	2	cut from pattern	½″ birch
B	Body	1	cut from pattern	¾″ birch
C	Rear wheel	1	4″ dia.	½″ birch
D	Axle	1	⅜″ dia. × 1½″	hardwood dowel
E	Rear legs	2	cut from pattern	½″ birch
F	Rear leg pivot	1	⅜″ dia. × 2⅞″	hardwood dowel
G	Front legs	2	cut from pattern	½″ birch
H	Wheels	2	1½″ dia.	hardwood wheel
I	Axle pegs	2	⁷⁄₃₂″ dia. × 1¼″	hardwood peg
J	Ears	2	cut from pattern	½″ birch
K	Ear pivot	1	⅜″ dia. × 1⅞″	hardwood dowel
L	Eyes	2	½″ dia. × ⅜″	walnut plug

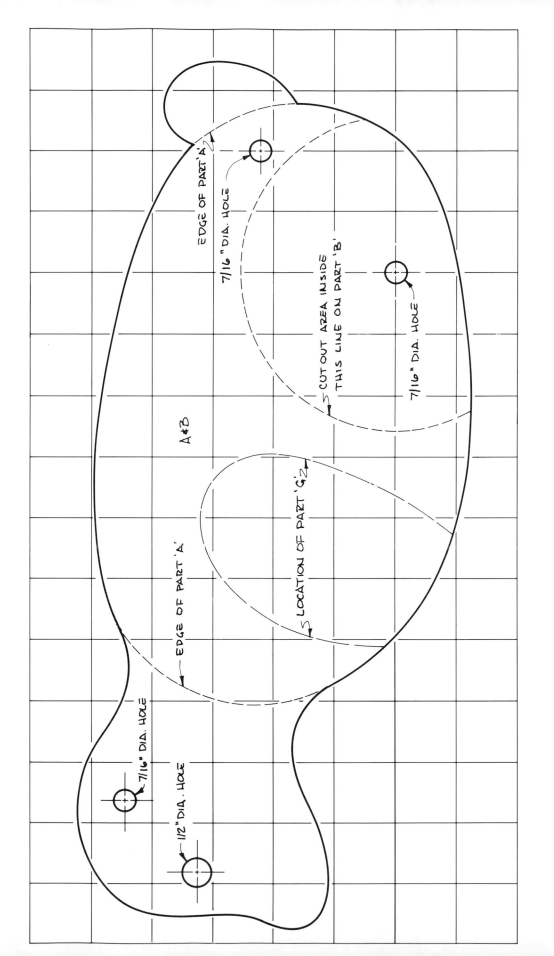

EDGE OF PART 'A'

7/16" DIA. HOLE

CUT OUT AREA INSIDE THIS LINE ON PART 'B'

7/16" DIA. HOLE

A & B

LOCATION OF PART 'C'

EDGE OF PART 'A'

7/16" DIA. HOLE

1/2" DIA. HOLE

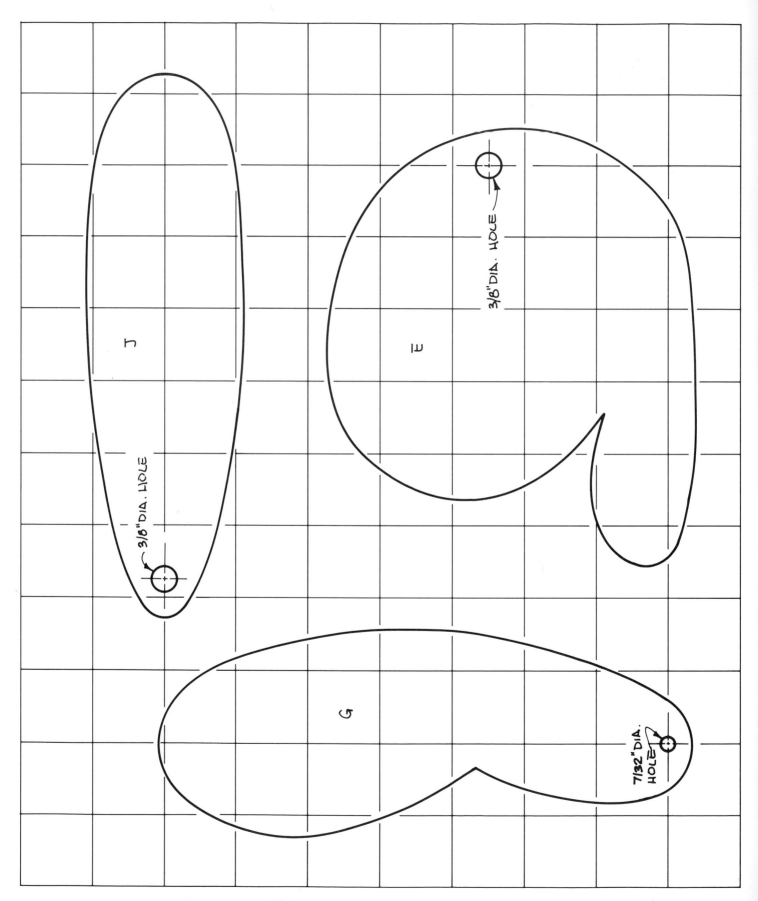

BOB CAT

Talk about a fat cat! Meet Bob—he's one happy fellow—with his big belly and playful face. Touch his tummy and he'll rock and roll and his head will bob back and forth. Bob Cat is a one-of-a-kind feline, sure to become a family favorite.

BEGIN CONSTRUCTION by enlarging the patterns for the head (A), body halves (B), spreaders (C), and tail halves (D). Edge-glue two ½"-thick walnut boards together to make a single board wide enough to make the body. Transfer these patterns to the walnut stock, then cut all parts to shape with a band or coping saw.

Use a router and a ¼" roundover bit to radius the edges of the head, body, and tail halves. Glue the tail halves to the body halves and when the glue has dried, sand the bottom edge smooth with #120 grit sandpaper.

Assemble the body by gluing the spreaders and body halves together. Check that the body halves are in alignment so the cat will sit squarely on a flat surface. After the glue has

dried, use a chisel to remove any excess that was squeezed out of the joints.

Mark the location of the nose (F) and eyes (H) on the head. Drill a ½" hole through the layout mark for the nose. Cut the nose from ½" hardwood dowel stock and insert it into the head. Mark the location of the whisker holes. Remove the nose and drill these ⅛" holes. Glue the nose in place, check-

ing that the whisker holes are placed so the whiskers will be in the proper position.

Glue the plastic eyes in place, then finish Bob with several coats of oil. Cut his whiskers to length and glue them into the nose. Attach Bob's head to his body by screwing the block (E) to the end of his neck.

Shopping List

Quantity	Description
8 feet	½" × 6" walnut
1 foot	½"-dia. hardwood dowel
6 feet	plastic lacing
4	¾" plastic eye
2	1"-long #6 wood screw

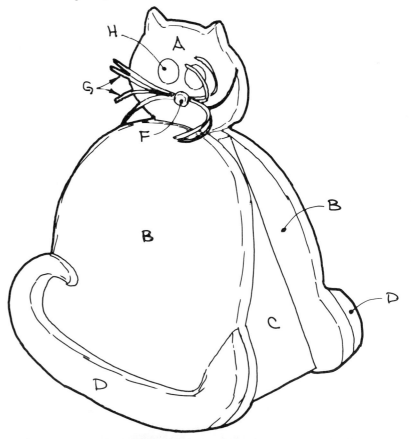

Parts List

Part	Name	No.	Size	Material
A	Head	1	cut from pattern	½″ walnut
B	Body halves	2	cut from pattern	½″ walnut
C	Spreaders	2	cut from pattern	½″ walnut
D	Tail halves	2	cut from pattern	½″ walnut
E	Block	1	½″ × 1½″ × 2″	walnut
F	Nose	1	½″ dia. × 1¼″	hardwood dowel
G	Whiskers	12	6″ long	plastic lacing
H	Eyes	4	¾″ dia.	plastic eye

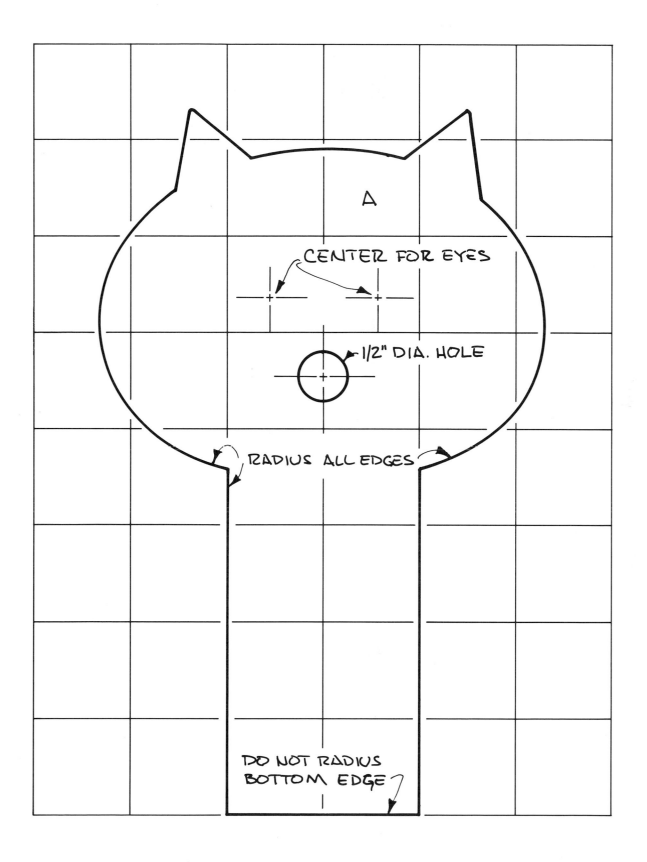

A

CENTER FOR EYES

1/2" DIA. HOLE

RADIUS ALL EDGES

DO NOT RADIUS
BOTTOM EDGE

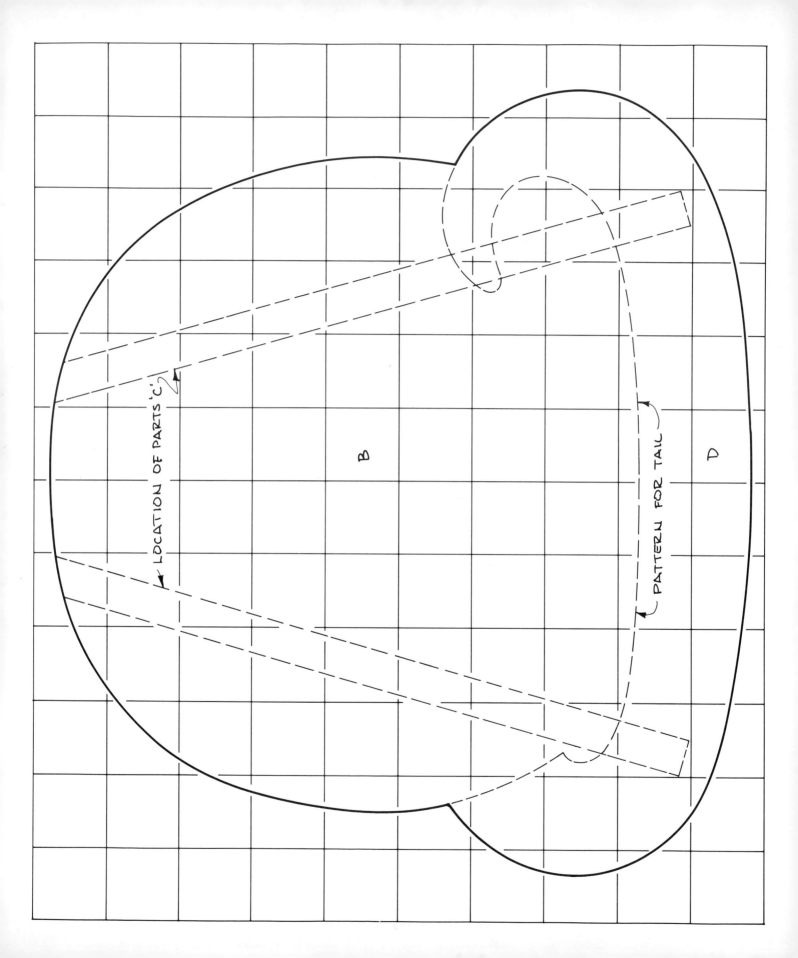

LOCATION OF PARTS 'C'

B

PATTERN FOR TAIL

D

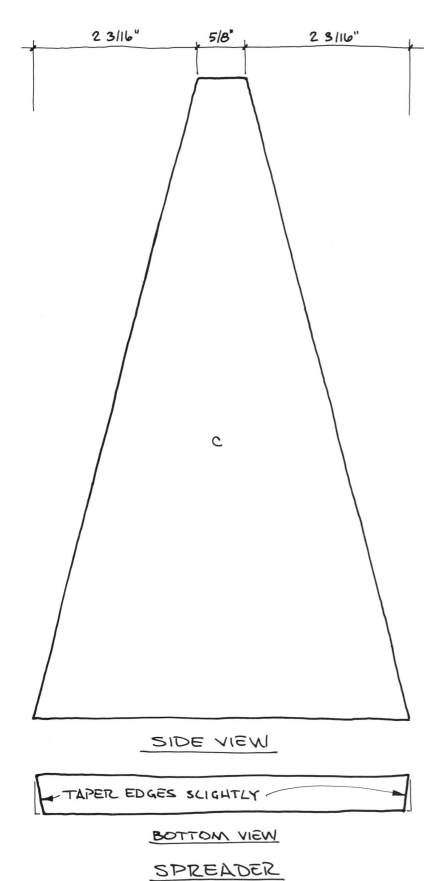

2 3/16"   5/8"   2 3/16"

C

SIDE VIEW

TAPER EDGES SLIGHTLY

BOTTOM VIEW

SPREADER

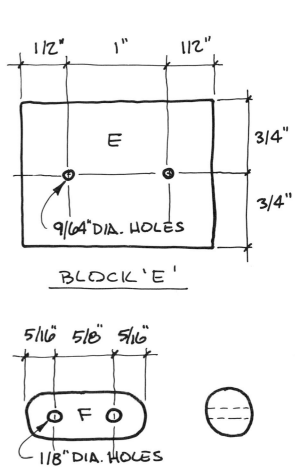

1/2"   1"   1/2"

E

3/4"

3/4"

9/64" DIA. HOLES

BLOCK 'E'

5/16" 5/8" 5/16"

F

1/8" DIA. HOLES

SIDE VIEW   END

NOSE 'F'

INFANT'S CRIB MOBILE

Sure to catch the inquisitive eyes of that precious new baby or toddler, these pretty birds are made of hardwood and veneer and attach sturdily to any crib.

Shopping List

Quantity	Description
1 foot	⅛″ × 4″ walnut
1 foot	4″-wide veneer
½″ foot	½″ × 3″ walnut
3 feet	¼″ hardwood dowel
4 feet	⅛″ hardwood dowel
1	8-20 × 1¼″ bolt, wing nut
1	spool dark thread
2 feet	½″ Velcro strap

BEGIN CONSTRUCTION with the crib bracket. Cut the bracket side (A), bracket top (B), and joint disks (D) from ½″ stock. Make the bracket pad (C) from scrap.

Glue the bracket side and top together. When the glue has dried, round over the edges of the bracket assembly and joint disks with a router and ¼″ roundover bit. If you don't have a router, sand all edges to break any sharp corners.

Make the upright (E) and arm (F) from ¼″ hardwood dowel stock and the bird dowels (I) from ⅛″ stock. Drill ¼″ holes for the upright and arm dowels in the bracket assembly and joint disks. Also drill ³⁄₁₆″ holes in the center of the joint disks for the locking bolt.

Enlarge the pattern for the bird body (G) and bird wing (H). Transfer the shape of the bird body to ⅛″ stock and the bird wing to veneer. Cut these to shape, then sand smooth with #220 grit sandpaper. Glue the wings to the body.

We finished the walnut base and dowels natural with a polyurethane varnish. Each bird is finished with a wipe-on tung oil finish.

Now the fun begins! Attach the bracket assembly to the crib with Velcro straps and insert the upright dowel. Place the joint assembly on top of the upright and insert the arm. From the end of the arm, hang the bird dowels and birds according to the plan or arrange them yourself. The birds hang by thread that is pushed into slits in the ends of the dowels. You will find it easier if you make the individual groupings of birds and balance them and then hang the smaller arrangements on the longer dowels.

Parts List

Part	Name	No.	Size	Material
A	Bracket side	1	½″ × 3″ × 3″	walnut
B	Bracket top	1	½″ × 1½″ × 3″	walnut
C	Bracket pad	1	¼″ × ¾″ × 1″	walnut
D	Joint disks	2	½″ × 1½″ dia	walnut
E	Upright	1	¼″ dia. × 16″	hardwood dowel
F	Arm	1	¼″ dia. × 20″	hardwood dowel
G	Bird body	7	cut from pattern	⅛″ hardwood
H	Bird wing	7	cut from pattern	hardwood veneer
I	Bird dowels	3	cut from pattern	⅛″-dia. dowel

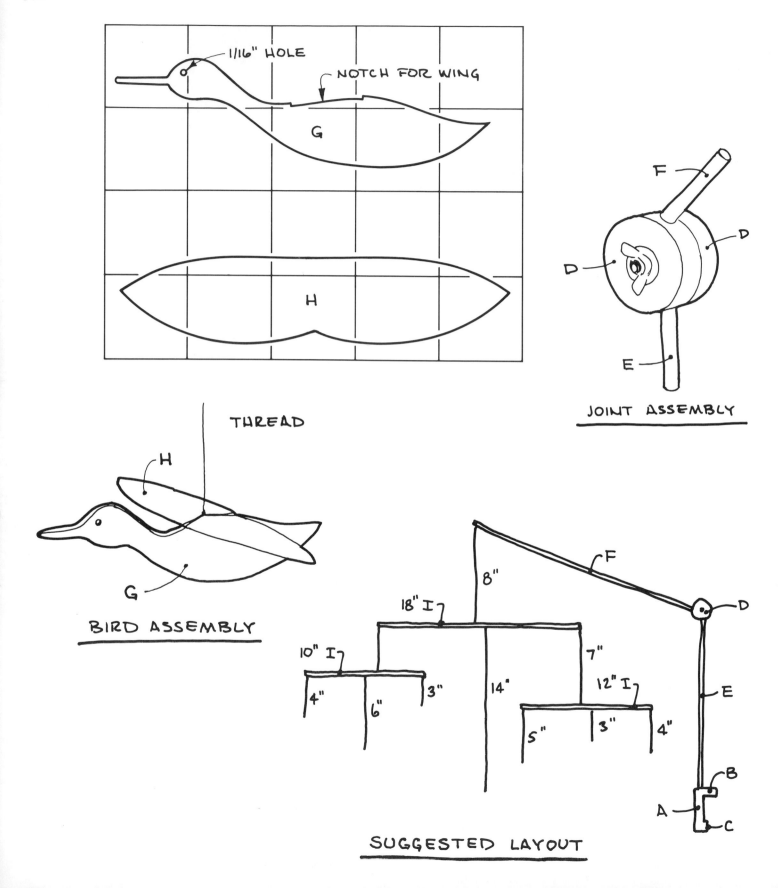

1/16" HOLE

NOTCH FOR WING

G

H

F

D

D

E

JOINT ASSEMBLY

THREAD

H

G

BIRD ASSEMBLY

8"

18" I

10" I

4"

6"

3"

14"

7"

12" I

5"

3"

4"

F

D

E

B

A

C

SUGGESTED LAYOUT

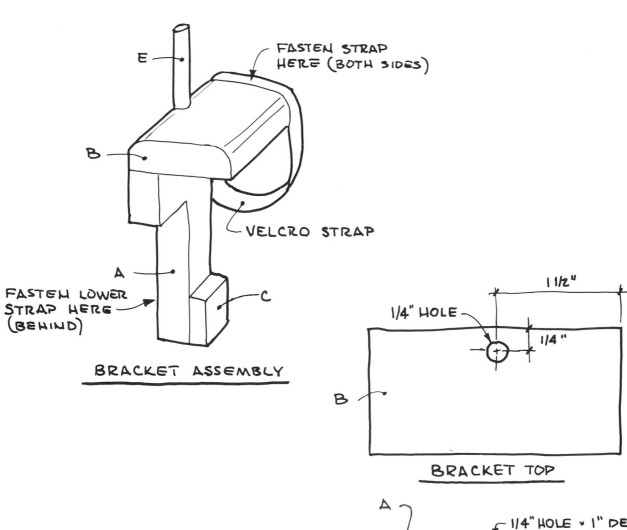

E

FASTEN STRAP HERE (BOTH SIDES)

B

VELCRO STRAP

A

FASTEN LOWER STRAP HERE (BEHIND)

C

BRACKET ASSEMBLY

1/4" HOLE

1 1/2"

1/4"

B

BRACKET TOP

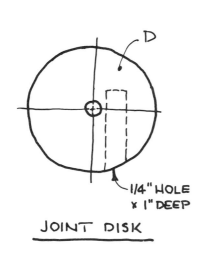

D

1/4" HOLE × 1" DEEP

JOINT DISK

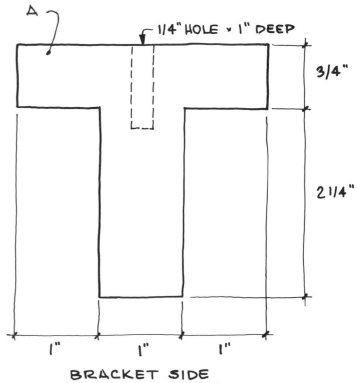

A

1/4" HOLE × 1" DEEP

3/4"

2 1/4"

1"   1"   1"

BRACKET SIDE

BEANBAG TOSS

Kids of all ages will enjoy the challenge of getting the bag in the bins of our simple-to-construct beanbag game board.

BEGIN CONSTRUCTION by cutting the game board (A), doors (D), and closure (E) to size from ½"-thick chipboard. Make the sides (B) and (C) from ¾" pine stock and the triangles (H), (I), (J), and (K) and bull's-eye parts (L) and (M) from ½" pine stock.

Pair up the triangles and glue and nail them together using 1" wire brads. Assemble the bull's-eye by nailing and gluing the bull's-eye tops and bottoms together. When the glue is dry, glue and nail a #2 triangle to the ends of the bull's-eye top.

Lay out the location of the beanbag bins and handhold on the game board. Note that all layout lines are measured from the two center diagonals. Mark these diagonals on the game board, then measure from the diagonals and draw the other layout lines according to the plan. After you have marked the location of the bins on the board, drill four pilot holes for the bin mounting screws through these lines.

Form the handhold by drilling 1" holes at both ends of the handhold layout. Then remove the area between these holes with a saw to form a slot. Sand the edges smooth with #120 grit sandpaper.

Shopping List

Quantity	Description
4 feet	½" × 4" pine
6 feet	½" × 6" pine
8 feet	1 × 6 pine
1	sheet (4 × 8) ½" chipboard
1	⅜"-dia. hardwood dowel
100	1¼"-long #6 FH wood screw
8	1½" × 1½" hinge and screws
2	screw eyes
2	1¾" screw hook
1 set	1" vinyl numbers

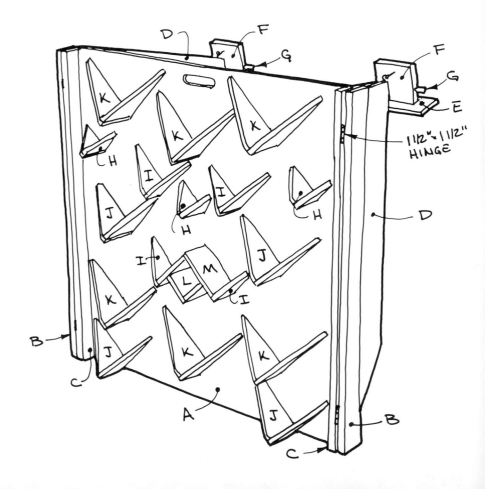

Put each bin in position against the game board and mark the location of its mounting screws on the bin edge with a pencil. Use the board pilot holes as a guide. Then drill screw pilot holes in the bins and screw and glue them to the game board.

Glue and screw narrow sides (C) to the face of the game board flush with the outside edge. Attach the wide sides (B) to the doors (D) with hinges screwed to the edges of the wide sides and to the back of the doors. Attach the wide and narrow sides together with hinges screwed to their outside faces. This arrangement allows the doors to close over the bins but enables them to fold back behind the game board to provide stand-up support.

Make the pegs (G) from ⅜" dowel stock, then drill holes in the blocks (F) for them. The peg locks into a hole in the upper and lower center bins to hold the closure assembly in place. The closure keeps the doors shut for carrying and storage. When the game board is in use the closure holds the doors together behind the board.

Drill a hole in the **V** of the center two large bins according to the plan. Place blocks (F) in position in the holes in the bins, then put the closure in place and align it with the top edge of the doors and mark the location of the blocks. Remove the closure and blocks, drill pilot holes through the closure, and mount the blocks to the closure with screws and glue.

Install the eyes (N) in the upper edge of the doors and the hooks in the sides of the blocks.

We used 1" vinyl numbers that are adhesive-backed and stick onto the game board. The highest score wins!

To make beanbags you need ¼ yard of 45"-wide cotton material folded lengthwise and 1 lb. Northern beans.

Cut eight 4" squares on the folded material. With right sides together sew around the square using ½" seam allowance. Leave a 1" opening.

Clip the four corners and turn right-side out and press. Fill bag with beans (or green peas) and use a running stitch to hand sew the opening closed.

Parts List

Part	Name	No.	Size	Material
A	Game board	1	½" × 34" × 34"	chipboard
B	Wide sides	2	¾" × 2½" × 34"	pine
C	Narrow sides	2	¾" × 1½" × 34"	pine
D	Doors	2	½" × 16⅝" × 34"	chipboard
E	Closure	1	½" × 3" × 28"	chipboard
F	Blocks	2	¾" × 4" × 4"	pine
G	Pegs	2	⅜" dia. × 3"	hardwood dowel
H	#1 Triangles	6	½" × 3" × 3"	pine
I	#2 Triangles	6	½" × 3" × 5"	pine
J	#3 Triangles	8	½" × 4" × 6"	pine
K	#4 Triangles	12	½" × 4" × 7"	pine
L	Bull's-eye bottoms	2	½" × 3" × 3½"	pine
M	Bull's-eye tops	2	½" × 3" × 5"	pine
N	Eyes	2	1"	steel eye
O	Hooks	2	1¾"	steel hook

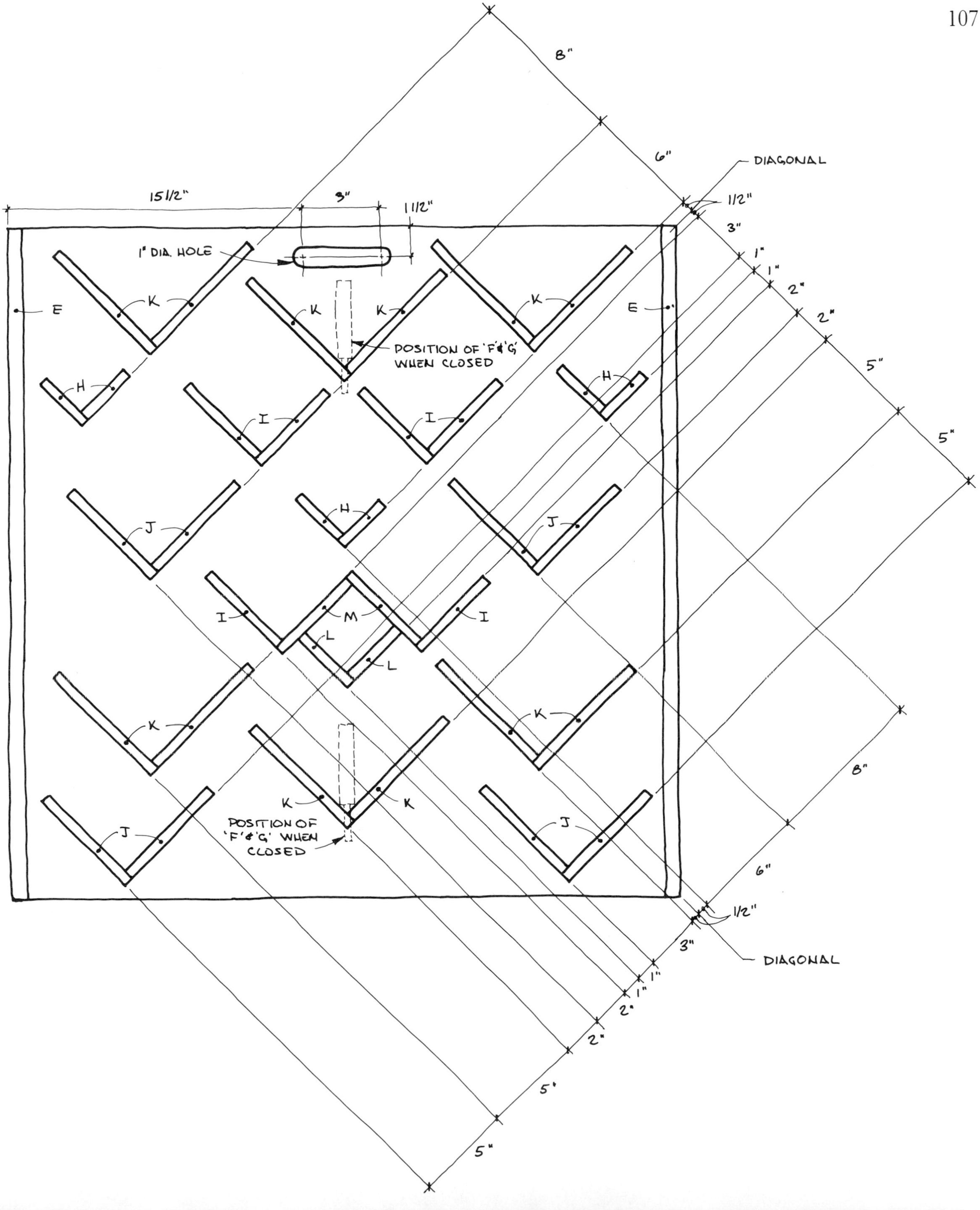

151/2"

8"

6"

DIAGONAL

3"

11/2"

1/2"

3"

1" DIA. HOLE

1"

1"

2"

2"

E

K

K

K

K

E

5"

POSITION OF 'F'&'G' WHEN CLOSED

H

H

5"

I

I

J

H

J

I

M

I

L

L

8"

K

K

6"

1/2"

K

K

3"

POSITION OF 'F'&'G' WHEN CLOSED

DIAGONAL

J

J

1"

1"

2"

2"

2"

5"

5"

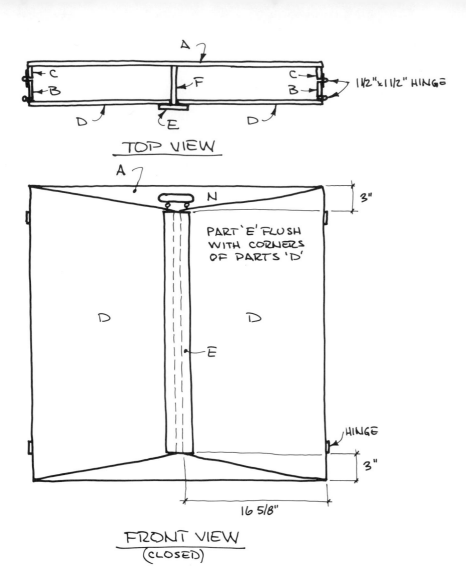

A

C
B
F
C
B
1 1/2" x 1 1/2" HINGE
D
E
D

TOP VIEW

A

N
3"

PART 'E' FLUSH
WITH CORNERS
OF PARTS 'D'

D
D

E

HINGE
3"

16 5/8"

FRONT VIEW
(CLOSED)

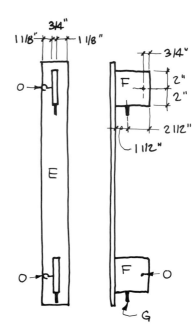

3/4"
1 1/8"   1 1/8"
3/4"
O
F
2"
2"
2 1/2"
1 1/2"
E
O
O
F
O
G

BACK VIEW   SIDE VIEW

CLOSURE

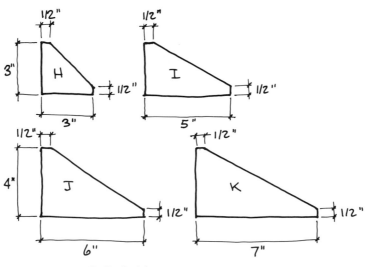

1/2"
1/2"
3"
H
1/2"
I
1/2"
3"
5"

1/2"
1/2"
4"
J
1/2"
K
1/2"
6"
7"

TRIANGLE DETAILS

TICK-TACK-TOE

One board game is good, but two are much better! Play both tick-tack-toe and checkers on this double-sided game board with hardwood pieces and checkers. You'll never have missing pieces because they all store handily between the boards.

BEGIN CONSTRUCTION with the board frame. Cut the ¾″ stock to a 1½″ width for the sides/back (A). Make the two ¼″ × ⅜″ grooves for the boards in the long piece before you cut the individual pieces to length. Do the same with the front pieces (B), cutting them square. Make the groove and then cut to length.

Make a 45-degree miter cut at each end of the frame parts. Arrange them for best fit and mark the parts so you can assemble them in the proper order.

Cut the game boards (C) and (F) to size and test their fit with the frame parts. If the boards are oversized the miter joints will not come together; trim if necessary.

Lay out and cut ¼″ × ⅛″-deep

grooves in the top surface of the Tick-Tack-Toe board for the long (D) and short (E) dividers. Cut the dividers to size and test their fit in the grooves.

Assemble the frame and the Tick-Tack-Toe board. Note that one front (B) forms the frame and is glued to the sides and board; the other is glued only to the checkerboard. Apply glue to all joints and assemble.

We used contact paper to help form the checker squares. Apply the paper to the face of the checkerboard and smooth it carefully. Mark the checkerboard grid on the contact paper. Note

that the row next to the board edge is 1⅝″ wide, all other rows are 1¼″ wide. Carefully cut out every other square and remove the paper from the squares, exposing the wood. Use a stick and rub it around the edge of each square to assure the contact paper is secure.

Apply a small amount of stain to a rag and dab it into the open squares. Do not try to apply a heavy coat of stain because it will seep under the paper. Instead apply several light coats. When the stain is dry remove the contact paper.

Slip the checkerboard into the frame

Shopping List

Quantity	Description
2 feet	1 × 4 walnut
4 feet	½″ × 4″ walnut
1	¼″ × 12″ × 24″ birch plywood
1 foot	1″ walnut dowel
1 foot	1″ birch dowel

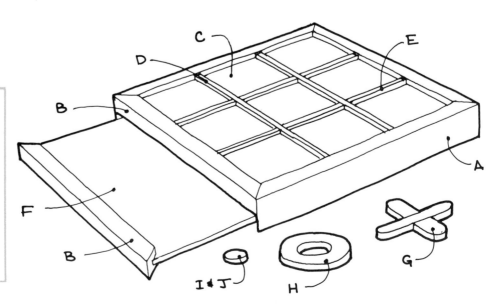

Parts List

Part	Name	No.	Size	Material
A	Sides/backs	3	¾" × 1½" × 11⁹⁄₁₆"	walnut
B	Fronts	2	¾" × ¾" × 11⁹⁄₁₆"	walnut
C	Tic-Tac-Toe board	1	¼" × 10¹³⁄₁₆" × 10¹³⁄₁₆"	birch plywood
D	Long dividers	2	¼" × ¼" × 10¹⁄₁₆"	walnut
E	Short dividers	6	¼" × ¼" × 3³⁄₁₆"	walnut
F	Checkerboard	1	¼" × 10¾" × 10¾"	birch plywood
G	Tic-Tac-Toe **X**	10	½" × ¾" × 3¾"	walnut
H	Tic-Tac-Toe **O**	5	½" × 2¾" dia.	walnut
I	Checkers	12	1" dia. × ⅜" thick	birch dowel
J	Checkers	12	1" dia. × ⅜" thick	walnut dowel

and glue on the front. Check the alignment of the front miter with the frame and remove the checkerboard and allow both parts to dry.

Cut and fit the long dividers into the grooves in the Tick-Tack-Toe board. Then fit and glue the short dividers. After the glue has dried, remove any excess with a sharp chisel and sand the frame and dividers with #120 grit sandpaper.

The **O** and **X** for the Tick-Tack-Toe game are easy to make. Use a coping saw or hole cutter to make the **O**. Cut the disk first, then cut out the center. The two halves of the **X** are joined with a lap joint. Make the checkers by slicing off ⅜″ sections of a 1″-dia. dowel.

After you have cut out and glued up parts, check that they slip into the storage area between the boards. If your ½″ stock is oversize, sand the pieces until they fit, then sand all edges smooth.

We finished the game board and pieces with several coats of low-luster polyurethane varnish.

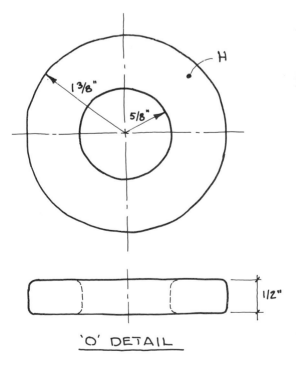

'O' DETAIL

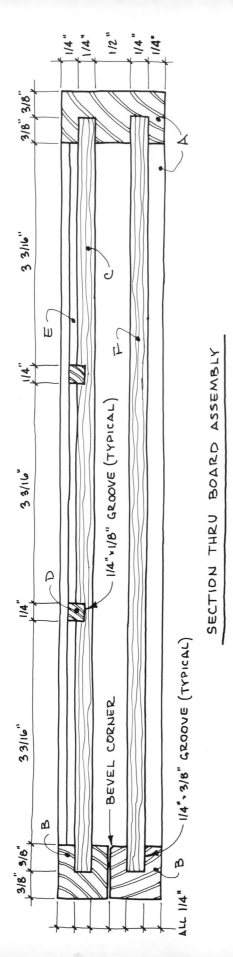

ALL 1/4"

1/4" × 3/8" GROOVE (TYPICAL)

1/4" × 1/8" GROOVE (TYPICAL)

BEVEL CORNER

SECTION THRU BOARD ASSEMBLY

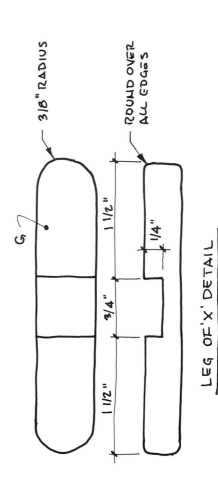

3/8" RADIUS

ROUND OVER ALL EDGES

LEG OF 'X' DETAIL

CHINESE CHECKERS

This game has been a family favorite for generations. It's the perfect rainy-day game for anyone and is as easy to play as it is to build. March 60 colorful markers from hole to hole across the unique hexagon-shaped board.

BEGIN CONSTRUCTION by gluing two pieces of 1 × 10 pine lumber to form an 18½"-wide board. Cut the board (A) to shape from this piece.

Enlarge the hole pattern on a piece of paper and tape it to the board. Use a nail set as a punch to transfer the hole locations to the board. Place the tip of the nail set on the layout marks and then hit it with your hammer to make a dent in the wood.

After all the hole locations have been transferred to the board, remove the pattern and drill the ¾" holes. Wrap tape around your drill to act as a depth gauge so all the holes will be exactly ½" deep.

When you have drilled all the holes, sand the board with #120 grit sandpaper and apply several coats of low-luster polyurethane varnish.

We used ready-made men (B), but if you have a lathe, you can turn your own. Be sure that they slip into the holes easily. Sand the men smooth with #220 grit sandpaper.

It is easy to paint the men if you make a platform to hold them while the paint dries. To make a platform drive #4d finish nails through a piece of scrap wood so the point of the nail sticks out of the back. Turn the board over and place the men on the nails by gently tapping them in place with a hammer. The nails will hold the men upright while you paint.

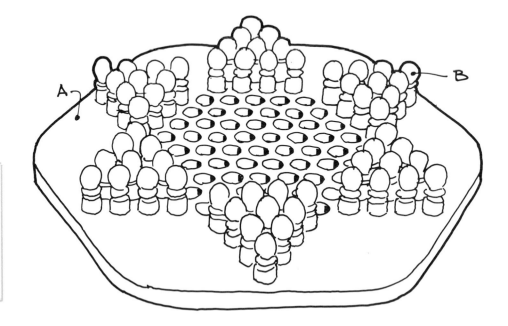

Shopping List

Quantity	Description
4 feet	1 × 10 pine
60	Preturned hardwood men

Parts List

Part	Name	No.	Size	Material
A	Board	1	¾″ × 15½″ × 16¹³⁄₁₆″	pine
B	Men	60	¾″ dia. × 2¼″	hardwood people

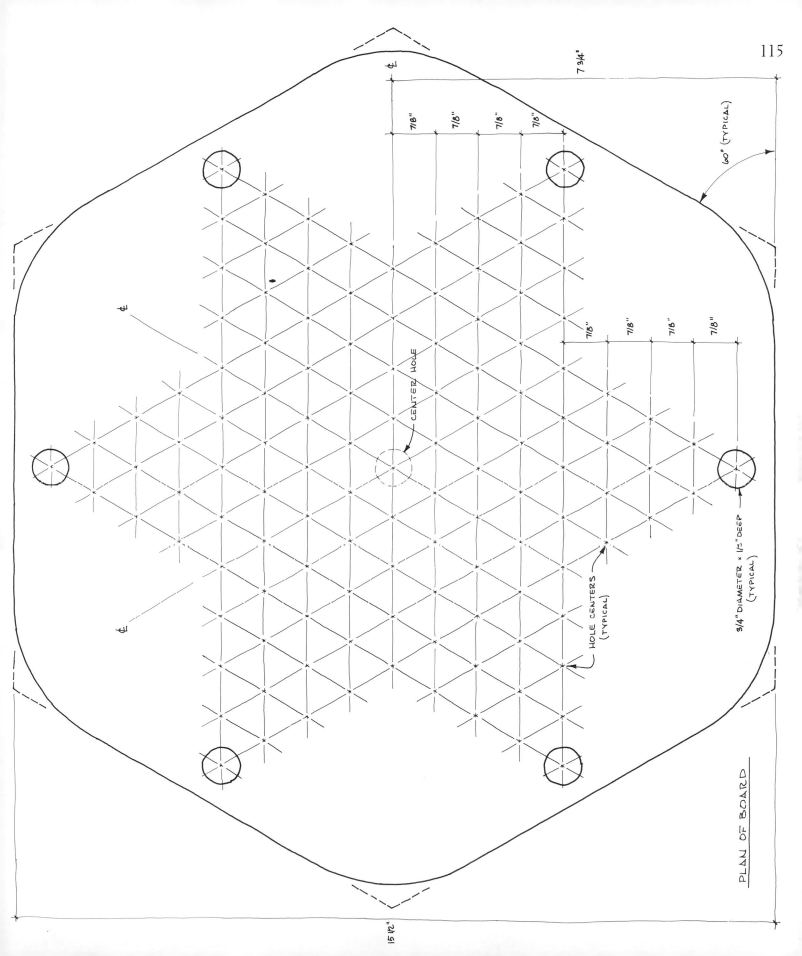

7 3/4"

60° (TYPICAL)

7/8" 7/8" 7/8" 7/8"

7/8" 7/8" 7/8" 7/8"

CENTER HOLE

HOLE CENTERS
(TYPICAL)

3/4" DIAMETER × 1/2" DEEP
(TYPICAL)

15 1/2"

PLAN OF BOARD

LABYRINTH

Youngsters learn coordination skills and have fun while playing with this hardwood lap box labyrinth. It is a challenging game for older kids too. The Superball finds a path through the maze, bouncing and bumping along the way.

BEGIN CONSTRUCTION by cutting the sides (A) from ½" walnut stock. Rip the dividers (D–G) to width from ¼" walnut stock and then cut individual dividers to length.

Set up your saw or router to cut the ¼" × ¼" joint dado in the ends of the sides. Cut the same size groove in the lower edge of the sides to receive the bottom (B). Cut a ¹⁄₁₆" × ¼"-deep groove in the inside face of the sides ⁵⁄₁₆" down from their top edge for the clear acrylic top (C).

Cut the top to size from acrylic window glazing. Assemble the top and sides without glue. Check the fit of the top; if it is oversize it will not allow the side joints to fit properly.

Lightly sand the sides with #220 grit

sandpaper. Glue the sides and top together. Use two ¾" wire brads to reinforce each corner and hold them together while the glue dries.

Check the size of the bottom by measuring the actual box, then cut the bottom for an exact fit. Sand the divider pieces smooth with #220 grit sandpaper, taking care not to round the edges.

Lay out the shape of the labyrinth on the bottom, then glue the dividers in place. Apply oil to the labyrinth dividers and bottom. Sand the sides smooth and apply the oil finish. Do not get the finish on the acrylic top. Insert the Superball in the maze and attach the bottom with brass screws.

Shopping List

Quantity	Description
5 feet	½" × 1¾" walnut
7 feet	¼" × 1⅛" walnut
1	24" × 24" × ¼" birch plywood
1	13" × 13" acrylic glazing
1	1" Superball
8	¾" #4 FH wood screws (brass)

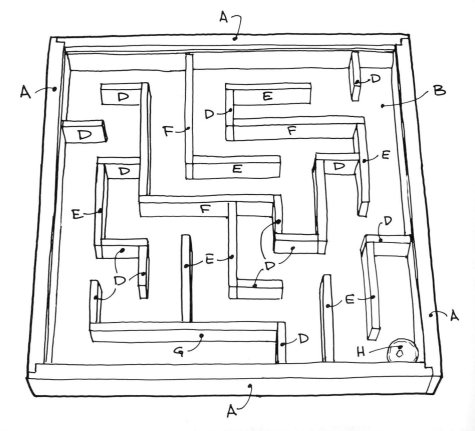

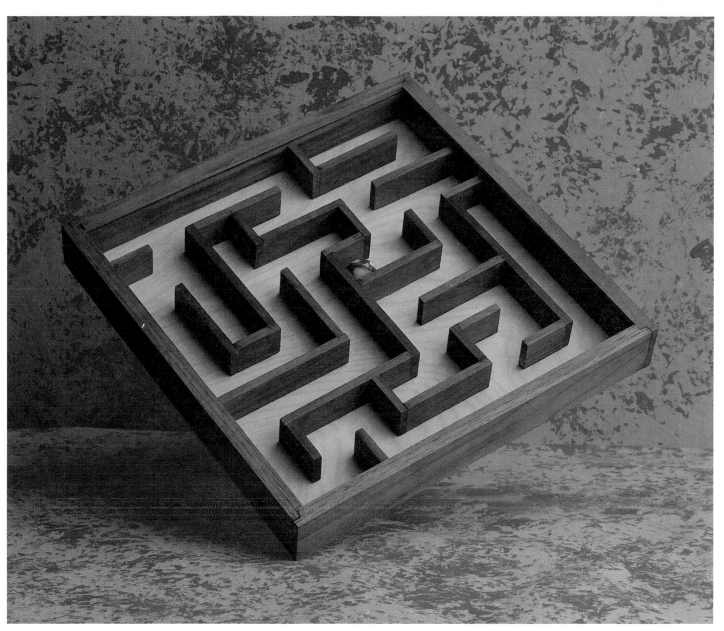

Parts List

Part	Name	No.	Size	Material
A	Sides	4	½″ × 1¾″ × 12½″	walnut
B	Bottom	1	¼″ × 12¼″ × 12¼″	birch plywood
C	Top	1	¹⁄₁₆″ × 12¼″ × 12¼″	acrylic
D	Dividers	14	¼″ × 1⅛″ × 1½″	walnut
E	Dividers	9	¼″ × 1⅛″ × 3″	walnut
F	Dividers	4	¼″ × 1⅛″ × 4½″	walnut
G	Divider	1	¼″ × 1⅛″ × 6″	walnut
H	Ball	1	1″ dia.	Superball

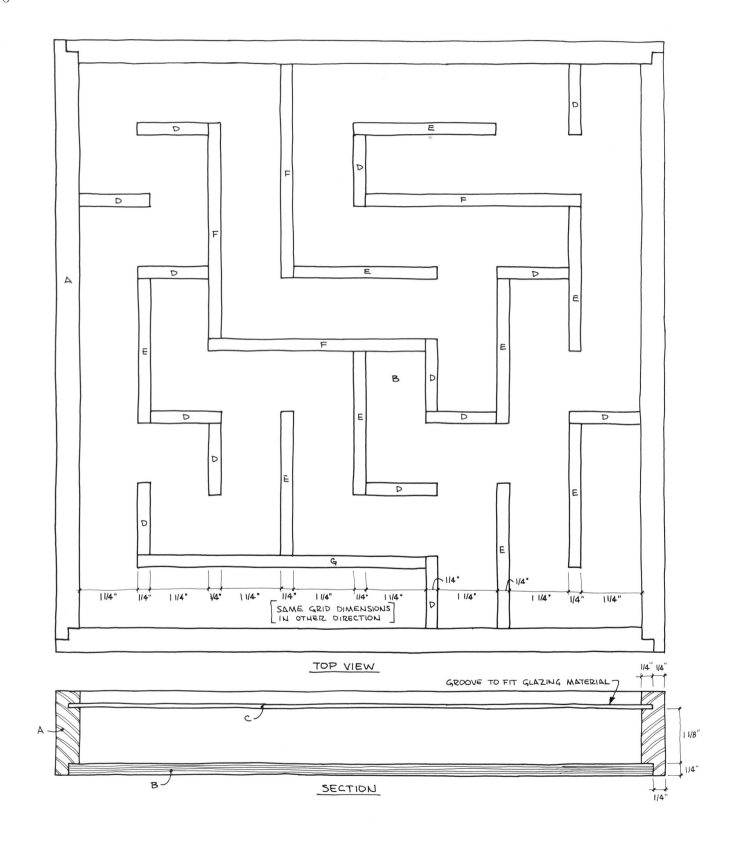

TOP VIEW

SECTION

GROOVE TO FIT GLAZING MATERIAL

SAME GRID DIMENSIONS
IN OTHER DIRECTION

1 1/4" 1/4" 1 1/4" 1/4" 1 1/4" 1/4" 1 1/4" 1/4" 1 1/4" 1 1/4" 1 1/4" 1/4" 1 1/4"

1/4" 1/4"
1 1/8"
1/4"
1/4"

GILDA THE GOOSE

Meet Gilda—our rollicking, frolicking goose! Make her waddle and toddle and move all about. You control her antics with a handheld crosspiece. Gilda is easy to build and quick to assemble using nylon rope for her neck and legs.

BEGIN CONSTRUCTION by transferring the patterns for the head (A), body (B) and feet (C) to the walnut stock. Cut these parts with a coping or band saw. Round all edges with a router and a ¼" roundover bit. If you do not have a router sand all parts with #120 grit sandpaper to ease the sharp edges.

Drill the ¼" holes for the neck and leg rope in the body, head, and foot according to the plan. Cut the foot (D) and body (E) controls from walnut scrap and glue together to form a cross. Drill ¹⁄₁₆" holes for the control strings in the feet, body, and head. Sand all parts with #220 grit sandpaper and apply a wipe-on oil finish.

Glue the neck rope to the body and head. Thread the leg rope through the hole in the body so that the legs are equal in length. Drive a ¾" wire brad through the bottom of the body into the leg rope to lock it in place. Glue the legs to the feet.

Now that Gilda is together, it's time to give her the power of movement. Cut the control lines from fishline and tie one end to Gilda's head, body, and feet. Thread the string from her head around the front of the body control and tie it off about 18" above the head. Run the string from the body to the end of the body control and tie the string off so Gilda's body is in a natural position with her head.

Lead the foot-control lines up to the foot control and tie them off so Gilda's bottom is about 3" from the ground. She is now ready to come to life—with a little practice, she will waddle right off your workbench!

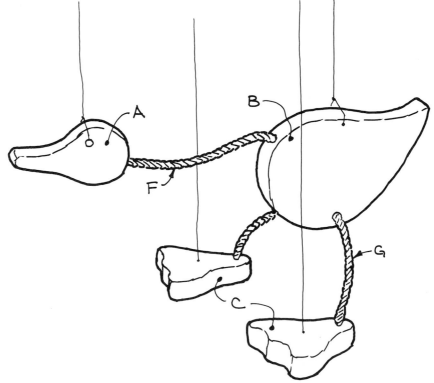

Shopping List

Quantity	Description
1 foot	¾" × 5½" (1 × 6) walnut
1 foot	½" × 5½" walnut
3 feet	¼"-dia. nylon rope
10 feet	fishline

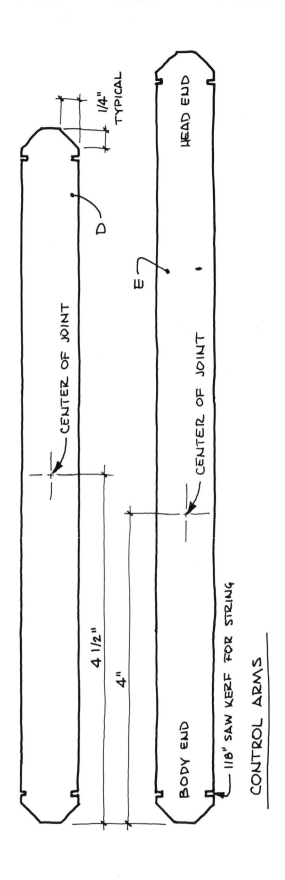

CONTROL ARMS

Parts List

Part	Name	No.	Size	Material
A	Head	1	cut from pattern	¾" walnut
B	Body	1	cut from pattern	¾" walnut
C	Feet	2	cut from pattern	½" walnut
D	Foot control	1	¼" × ¾" × 8"	walnut
E	Body control	1	¼" × ¾" × 10"	walnut
F	Neck	1	¼" dia.	nylon rope
G	Legs	1	¼" dia.	nylon rope

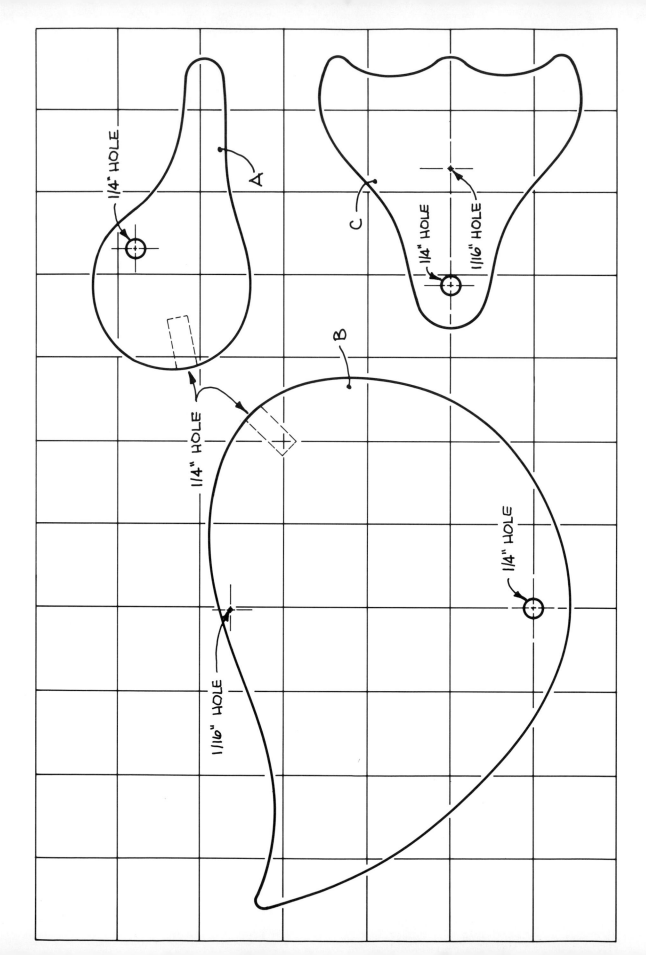

1/4" HOLE

A

C

1/4" HOLE

1/16" HOLE

1/4" HOLE

B

1/4" HOLE

1/16" HOLE

1/4" HOLE

SPINNING TOP

Wind it up and watch it whirl away! Our old-fashioned wooden top will delight children of all ages. The unique design makes it easy to build and fun to play with time and again.

BEGIN CONSTRUCTION of this simple project by cutting the handle (A) and arms (B) to size. Shape the arms with a coping or band saw or leave them square.

Glue the handle and arms together and clamp. If you don't have clamps, use some ⅝″ wire brads to hold the unit together while the glue dries.

The easiest way to make the top disk is to use a 3″-dia. hole cutter. You can also cut the disk with a coping or band saw. (Make several top disks as they will become worn and nicked with use.)

Drill a ⅜″ hole in the center for the top shaft (D).

Make the top shaft from ⅜″ dowel stock. Sand one end to a point, then glue the top shaft into the top disk. Cut the top cap (E) from 1″ dowel stock.

When the glue is dry, spin the top assembly and check for balance. Insert one end of the shaft into your electric drill and secure the drill to your bench. Then, with the top disk spinning, carefully sand it smooth.

Glue the top cap to the end of the top shaft, and when dry, sand all parts

with #120 grit sandpaper. Round all sharp edges and finish-sand with #220 grit paper. We applied several coats of a low-luster polyurethane varnish to the handle and a wipe-on oil finish to the top. Drill a 1/16″ hole in the center of the handle (F) and thread string through it, then tie it off.

To launch the top, just wrap string around the shaft. Hold the handle so the slot is facing away from you, place the top in the handle and pull the string. With a little practice you will be able to direct your spinning top exactly (well, almost) where you want it to land.

Shopping List
(All parts from scrap box)

Quantity	Description
6 inches	1 × 2 pine or hardwood
6 inches	½″ × 2″ pine or hardwood
6 inches	1 × 4 pine or hardwood
8 inches	⅜″-dia. hardwood dowel
6 inches	1″-dia. hardwood dowel
3 feet	string

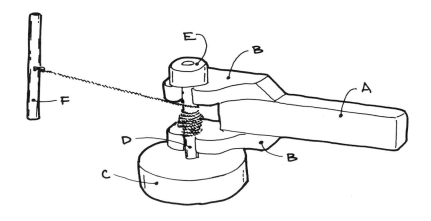

Parts List

Part	Name	No.	Size	Material
A	Handle	1	¾″ × 1″ × 5″	pine
B	Arms	2	cut to pattern	½″ pine
C	Top disk	1	3 ″ dia. × ¾″	walnut
D	Top shaft	1	⅜″ dia. × 4″	hardwood dowel
E	Top cap	1	1″ dia. × ½″	hardwood dowel
F	String handle	1	⅜″ dia. × 3″	hardwood dowel

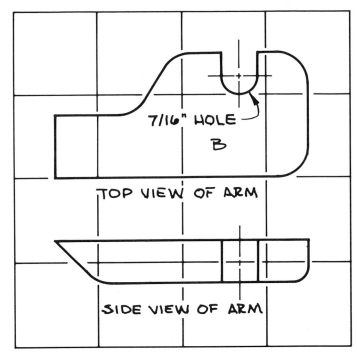

7/16" HOLE

B

TOP VIEW OF ARM

SIDE VIEW OF ARM

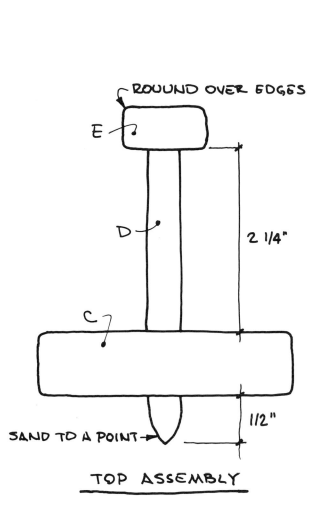

ROUND OVER EDGES

E

D

C

2 1/4"

1/2"

SAND TO A POINT →

TOP ASSEMBLY

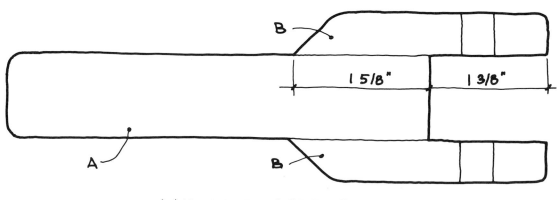

B

1 5/8"   1 3/8"

A

B

LAUNCHER ASSEMBLY

ABACUS

This three-dimensional abacus makes a game out of counting. Preschoolers learn to count colorful beads that slide on wooden dowels—and have fun in the process! It's a cinch to assemble.

BEGIN CONSTRUCTION by making the sides (A). Cut them from ¾" pine stock. The overall length specified in the parts list is to the tip of the miter; cut the parts slightly longer and then trim them back when making the 30-degree miter on each end. After you cut the miters, match up the parts for best fit.

Use a coping saw to make the disks (B) out of ¼" stock. You can also make these by cutting off ¼"-thick pieces of a large dowel.

Glue the triangles and disks to-

gether, using ⅝" wire brads to hold the joints tight until the glue dries. When dry, use a sharp chisel to remove excess glue and cut off the triangle points. Sand all edges and grind the ends of the triangle to match the radius of the disks.

Lay out and drill the ⁵⁄₁₆" holes for the rods (C). They should be at least ⅜" deep. Wrap tape around your drill as a gauge to help you drill all the holes to the same depth.

Cut the rods to length and glue them into one side of the abacus. Finish-

sand both sides and the dowels with #220 grit sandpaper. When the glue is dry, remove any excess that has been squeezed out.

We applied a wipe-on tung oil finish. Keep the finish off the last ¼" of the dowel rods and out of the rod holes.

When the finish is dry slip on the beads (D). Apply glue to the rod holes sparingly and assemble the abacus. Tap the side to fully seat the dowel rods and place on a flat surface until the glue has set.

Shopping List

Quantity	Description
6 feet	¾" × 1" pine
1 foot	¼" × 1½ × pine lattice
5	⁵⁄₁₆" dia. × 36" hardwood dowel
100	1" beads (⅜" hole)

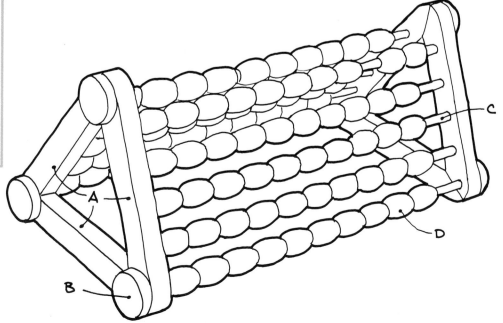

Parts List

Part	Name	No.	Size	Material
A	Sides	6	¾″ × 1″ × 8½″	pine
B	Disks	6	1½″ dia. × ¼″	hardwood dowel
C	Rods	10	⁵⁄₁₆″ dia. × 14¾″	hardwood dowel
D	Beads	100	1″ long, ⅜″ hole	hardwood beads

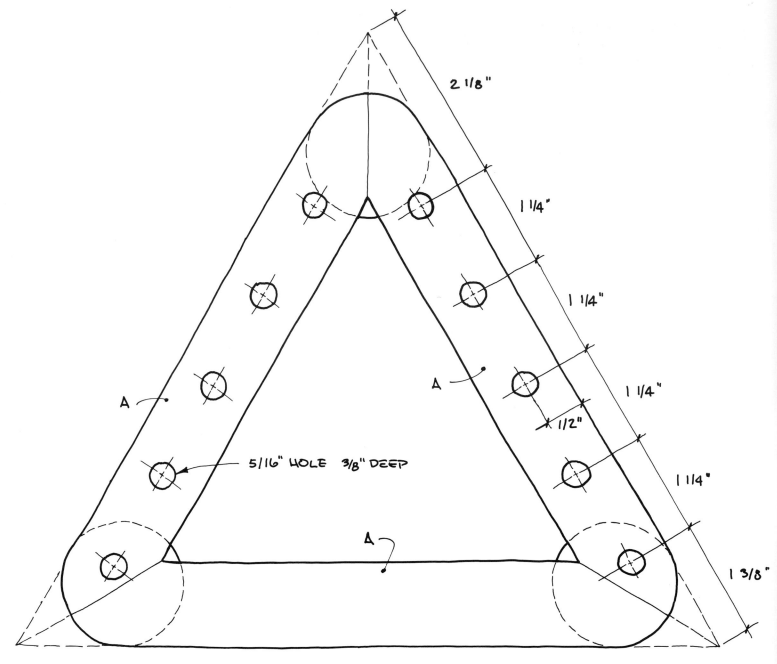

2 1/8"

1 1/4"

1 1/4"

1 1/4"

1/2"

1 1/4"

1 3/8"

A

A

A

5/16" HOLE   3/8" DEEP

SIDE DETAIL

CONSTRUCTION BLOCKS

Tucked inside our bulging red bag your budding young builder finds a stash of building blocks to enjoy. This just-for-fun sack of hardwood building parts keeps even the most active youngsters occupied—and all the parts store handily in the sack when playtime is over.

BEGIN CONSTRUCTION by cutting the ¾″ stock into 1½″-wide strips. Then cut blocks (A–E) to length. If you purchased 2 × 2 stock for blocks (F–J) cut these to length. Otherwise cut the 1½″-thick stock into 1½″-wide strips and cut off pieces to form the blocks.

Make the rods from hardwood dowels. Then sand the cut ends smooth with #120 grit sandpaper. Sand all sharp edges of the blocks smooth and apply a light coat of mineral oil as a finish.

To make the sack buy ¾ yd. of 45″-wide sturdy cotton fabric. Fold mate-

Shopping List

Quantity	Description
12 feet	1 × 2 birch
12 feet	2 × 2 birch
6 feet	¾″-dia. hardwood dowel
6 feet	1″-dia. hardwood dowel

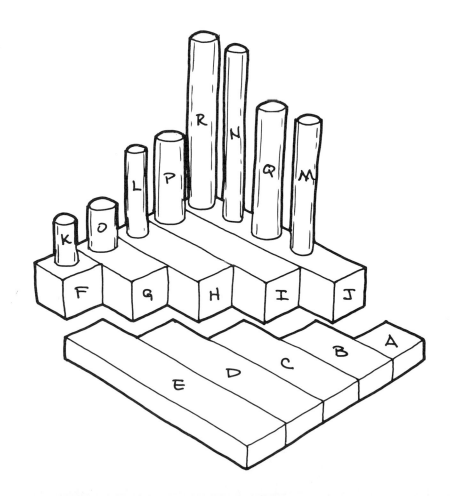

rial crosswise and cut piece of fabric 20″ × 21″. Stitch two sides using a ⅝″ seam allowance. (Double-stitch all seams throughout.) Clip corners and turn. Turn under unsewn top ½″. Press and stitch. Turn under 1½″ to form casing. Make two 1″ buttonholes in either side of sack 1½″ from top. Stitch casing down.

Cut two straps 2½″ × 19½″. Sew with ½″ seam allowance. Run through buttonhole openings. Stitch ends closed (or use ribbon or light rope for ties).

Parts List

Part	Name	No.	Size	Material
A	Blocks	8	¾″ × 1½″ × 1½″	birch
B	Blocks	8	¾″ × 1½″ × 3″	birch
C	Blocks	6ʻ	¾″ × 1½″ × 4½″.	birch
D	Blocks	6	¾″ × 1½″ × 6″	birch
E	Blocks	4	¾″ × 1½″ × 7½″	birch
F	Blocks	8	1½″ × 1½″ × 1½″	birch
G	Blocks	8	1½″ × 1½″ × 3″	birch
H	Blocks	6	1½″ × 1½″ × 4½″	birch
I.	Blocks	6	1½″ × 1½″ × 6″	birch
J	Blocks	4	1½″ × 1½″ × 7½″	birch
K	Cylinders	4	¾″ dia × 1½″	birch dowel
L	Cylinders	4	¾″ dia. × 3″	birch dowel
M	Cylinders	4	¾″ dia. × 4½″	birch dowel
N	Cylinders	4	¾″ dia. × 6″	birch dowel
O	Cylinders	4	1″ dia. × 1½″	birch dowel
P	Cylinders	4	1″ dia. × 3″	birch dowel
Q	Cylinders	4	1″ dia. × 4½″	birch dowel
R	Cylinders	4	1″ dia. × 6″	birch dowel

PUZZLE BOARD CLOCK

"Five is bigger than three but smaller than seven" is the lesson a little one will learn playing with this clever clock. Segments of the clock in graduating sizes fit into place on its face, which has a rotating dial. It is easy to build and a good project for a first-time woodworker.

BEGIN CONSTRUCTION by drawing a 13"-dia. circle for the base (A) on a piece of ½" chipboard and carefully mark the center. Cut out the base with a saber or band saw.

Lay out the pattern for the segments (B) according to the drawing and transfer it to ¼" walnut stock and cut out the 12 wedge-shaped segments. Assemble the segments into the clock face and check the fit of each piece. Sand the edges of the segments that do not fit perfectly.

Using the pattern, mark the peg (F) holes on each segment and the arc that divides the stationary part from the removable part. Drill ⅜" holes through these peg marks. Cut the segments into two parts along the arcs with a coping or band saw.

Place the segments on the base and carefully align the pieces so they are

Shopping List

Quantity	Description
4 feet	½" × 6" walnut
1	½" chipboard scrap 13" × 13"
1 foot	¼" × 2" maple
1 foot	⅜"-dia. hardwood dowel
1 set	1" vinyl numbers

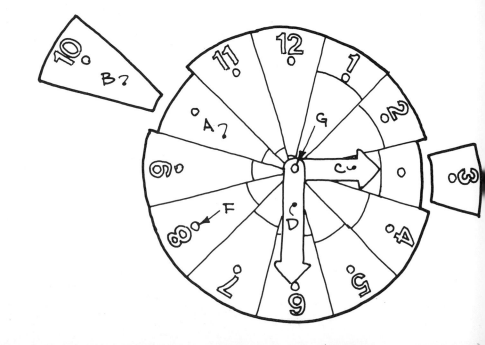

centered. Remove the center pieces and apply glue to their backs, then carefully replace them. After the center segment pieces are in place, check the alignment of all the parts before the glue sets.

Drill the holes for the pegs in the base by using the removable segments as a template. Drill a ⅜″ hole through the center of the clock for the pivot (G). Cut the pegs and pivot to length from ⅜″ dowel stock and glue them in place.

Transfer the shape of the hour hand (C), minute hand (D) and spacer (E) to maple and cut them to shape. Glue the spacer to the back of the hour hand.

Sand your clock with #220 grit sandpaper and then apply an oil finish. After the finish has dried, apply self-stick vinyl numbers to the segments and your puzzle clock is ready to tell time and teach numbers.

Parts List

Part	Name	No.	Size	Material
A	Base	1	½" × 13" dia.	chipboard
B	Segments	12	¼" × 3⅝" × 7" (radius)	walnut
C	Hour hand	1	¼" × 1⅝" × 4¾"	maple
D	Minute hand	1	¼" × 1⅝" × 5⅞"	maple
E	Spacer	1	¼" × 1¾" × 1"	maple
F	Pegs	12	⅜" dia. × ¾"	hardwood dowel
G	Pivot	1	⅜" dia. × 1¼"	hardwood dowel

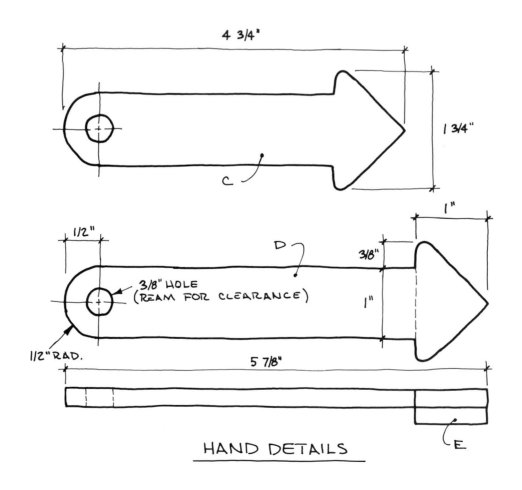

HAND DETAILS

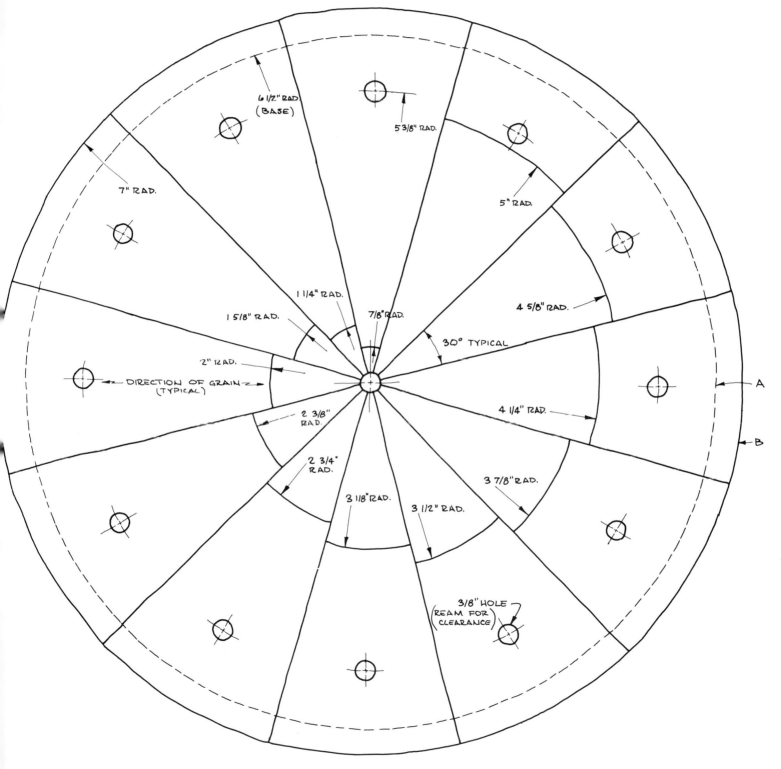

6 1/2" RAD. (BASE)

5 3/8" RAD.

7" RAD.

5" RAD.

1 1/4" RAD.

1 5/8" RAD.

7/8" RAD.

4 5/8" RAD.

30° TYPICAL

2" RAD.

DIRECTION OF GRAIN (TYPICAL)

A

2 3/8" RAD.

4 1/4" RAD.

B

2 3/4" RAD.

3 7/8" RAD.

3 1/8" RAD.

3 1/2" RAD.

3/8" HOLE (REAM FOR CLEARANCE)

PLAN OF FACE

POUNDING BENCH

Whack those pegs for a walloping good time! This hardwood bench is indestructible, so let your toddler pound away to his heart's content—he's acquiring valuable coordination skills.

BEGIN CONSTRUCTION by cutting the top (A), sides (B), and legs (C) from ¾"-thick walnut stock. Glue two pieces of ¾" walnut stock together to form the 1½" piece needed for the hammerhead (E). Make the pegs (D) from 1"-dia. hardwood dowel stock and the hammer handle from ⅝"-dia. stock.

After the hammerhead glue is dry, cut this laminate into an octagon with a band saw, or leave it a rectangle and round all sharp edges with #120 grit sandpaper. Bevel the front corners of the hammerhead to prevent it from splitting when your little carpenter starts pounding. Drill a ⅝" hole in the hammerhead to receive the hammer handle.

Lay out and drill the 1" holes for the pegs in the top. Sand all the bench parts smooth with #120 grit sandpaper and round all sharp edges.

Assemble the bench by gluing the one side and legs together, then glue the top to this assembly, sandwiching it between the halves of the other side. Check that the legs and sides are square with the top.

Sand the pegs smooth and sand a small bevel around their edges to make inserting them into the holes easier. Make saw cuts in the pegs according to the plan.

When all glue has dried chip off any excess with a chisel and apply a wipe-on oil finish.

Shopping List	
Quantity	**Description**
4 feet	1 × 8 walnut
3 feet	1"-dia. hardwood dowel
1 foot	⅝"-dia. hardwood dowel

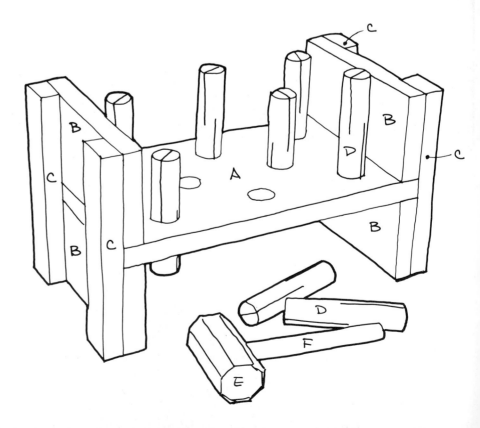

Parts List

Part	Name	No.	Size	Material
A	Top	1	¾″ × 7¼″ × 12½″	walnut
B	Sides	4	¾″ × 3½″ × 7¼″	walnut
C	Legs	4	¾″ × 1½″ × 7¾″	walnut
D	Pegs	8	1″ dia. × 4¼″	hardwood dowel
E	Hammerhead	1	1½″ × 1½″ × 3½″	walnut
F	Hammer handle	1	⅝″ dia. × 6″	hardwood dowel

138

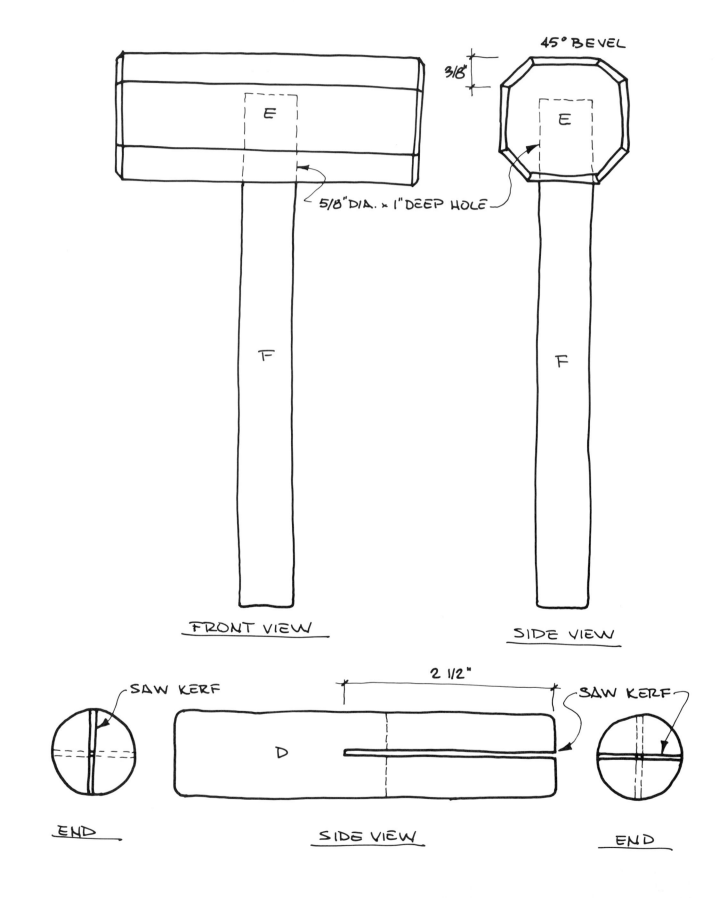

45° BEVEL

3/8"

E

E

5/8" DIA. x 1" DEEP HOLE

F

F

FRONT VIEW

SIDE VIEW

SAW KERF

2 1/2"

SAW KERF

D

END

SIDE VIEW

END

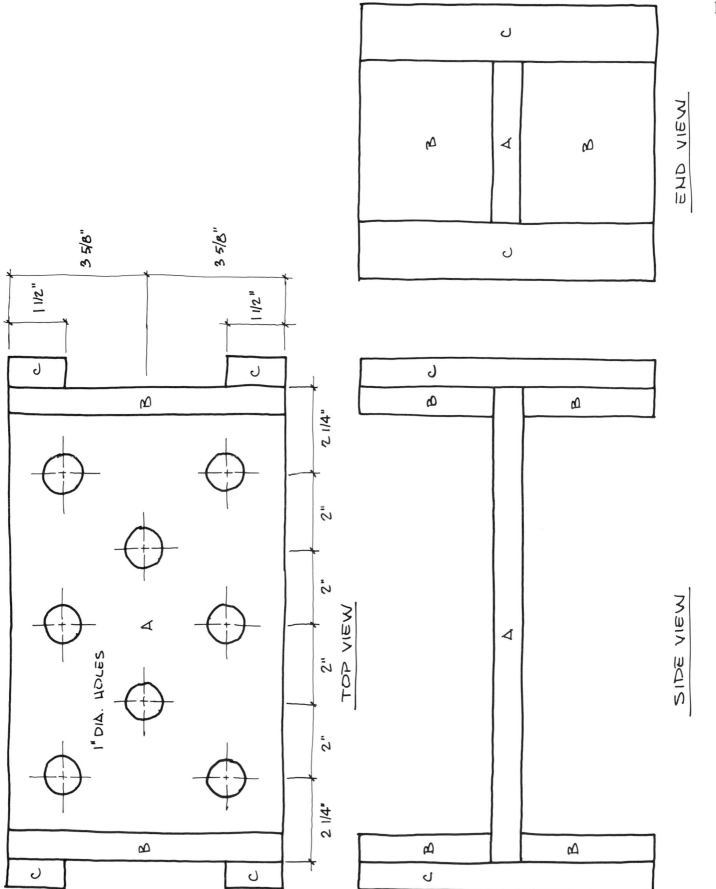

3 5/8"

3 5/8"

1 1/2"

1 1/2"

C

C

B

1" DIA. HOLES

A

B

C

C

2 1/4"

2"

2"

2"

2"

2 1/4"

TOP VIEW

C

B

A

B

C

END VIEW

C

B

A

B

C

SIDE VIEW

NAME PUZZLE

Our personalized puzzle is a toy that youngsters will never outgrow. As little folks they'll have fun learning to spell their name displayed in big bright letters. And as they get older, the puzzle becomes a nifty addition to their bedroom wall or shelf that they're proud to display.

BEGIN CONSTRUCTION of the name puzzle by tracing your child's name from the letter patterns. Lay out the letters to spell the name. Then measure the length of the name and add 2″ to this figure to get the length of the name board (A), back (B), and top/bottom (C).

Cut the name board to size from basswood plywood that can be purchased at most hobby shops. Make the back from acrylic glazing that you'll find sold at hardware stores. Cut the sides and ends (D) from ½″ pine stock.

Use a router or dado head and a table saw to make the ⅜″-wide ¼″-deep groove in the top/bottom and end parts for the name board and back. Cut this groove down the center of these parts, then make ¼″-deep, ½″-wide dado cuts in the ends of the top/bottom to form the corner joints.

Position the name pattern on the name board so the first and last letters are 1″ from the ends, then trace around the letters to transfer their shapes to the plywood. Cut out the letters with a band saw or jigsaw. Cut carefully. Remember, both the outside and inside letter will be used.

Use #120 grit sandpaper and lightly sand the inside edge of the letter cut-outs in the name board and the outer edge of the letters. Dust the name board carefully and apply finish. We used a satin polyurethane varnish.

When the finish is dry on the name board, sandwich it with the acrylic back and assemble the sides and ends with glue. Radius the outside corners of the frame with a router and a ¼″ round-over bit. Sand the frame smooth and paint.

Paint each letter with a bright primary color and your name puzzle is ready to challenge, teach, and be enjoyed.

Shopping List

Quantity	Description
3 feet	½″ × 3½″ pine
1	¼″ × 12″ × 24″ basswood plywood
1	¹⁄₁₆″ × 5″ × ¾″ acrylic glazing

Parts List				
Part	Name	No.	Size	Material
A	Name board	1	¼″ × 5″ × ***	basswood plywood
B	Back	1	¹⁄₁₆″ × 5″ × ***	acrylic glazing
C	Top/bottom	2	½″ × 1½″ ***	pine
D	Ends	2	½″ × 1½″ × 5½″	pine

***Note: Dimensions will vary with name.

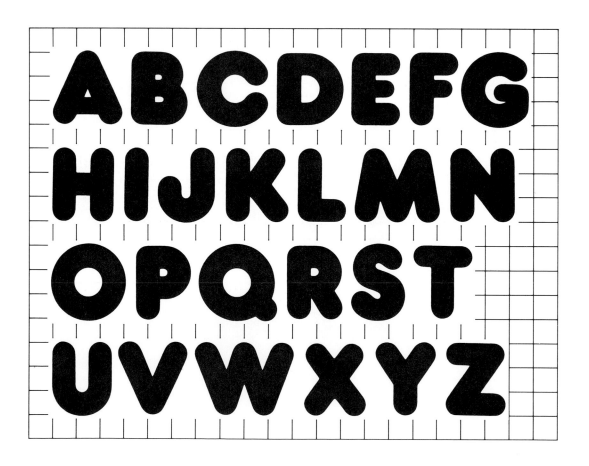

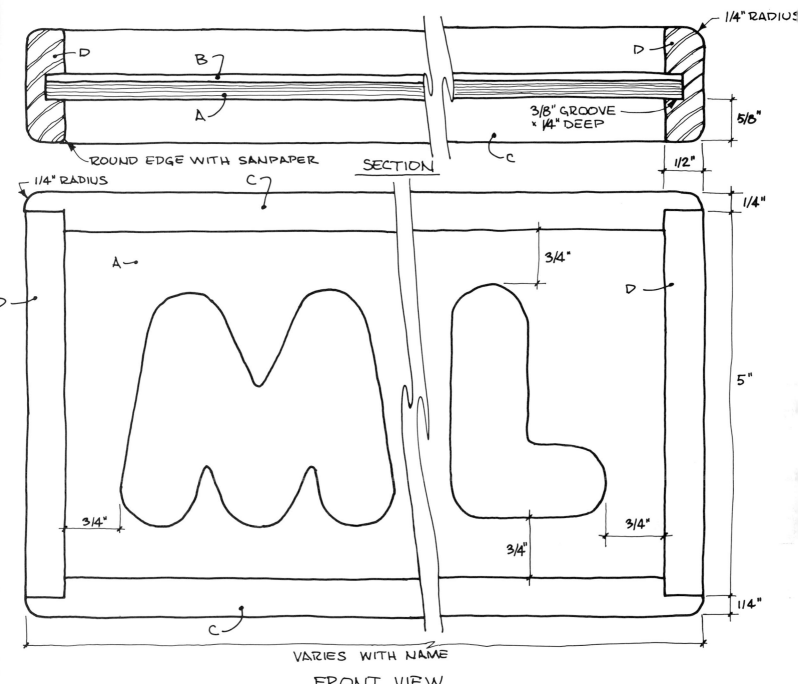

1/4" RADIUS

D

B

A

D

3/8" GROOVE
x 1/4" DEEP

5/8"

ROUND EDGE WITH SANPAPER

SECTION

C

1/2"

1/4" RADIUS

C

1/4"

A

3/4"

D

5"

3/4"

3/4"

3/4"

3/4"

C

1/4"

VARIES WITH NAME

FRONT VIEW

NUMBER RODS

Putting this game away is almost as much fun as taking it out to play. Youngsters learn number values the easy way by stacking, sorting, and building things with these hardwood rods, which fit into a customized board.

BEGIN CONSTRUCTION by cutting the wood into ½"-square strips. Check the thickness of the wood and the accuracy of your cut. If the rods are oversized, the error will be magnified many times since each one will be lined up next to the other one.

It is important that rods of the same number be the same length. After you have sized the rod stock, cut the individual rods to length. Begin with rod 1 (C), which is ½" long. Each rod grows by ½" until you finish with rod 10 (L), which is exactly 5" long.

Sand the rods lightly with #220 grit sandpaper, then arrange them according to the pattern to form a square. Measure the square accurately. If it is more than 10" increase the size of base (A) and sides (B) to provide at least ⅛" clearance between the rods and the sides.

Cut the base from ½" pine stock and make the sides from ¼" pine lattice. Lay out the rod pattern on the base with a light pencil line, then go over it with a paint pen, available at hobby stores.

Glue and nail the sides to the base with 1" wire brads. Fill their heads with wood filler, then sand the sides and base with #120 grit sandpaper.

To help youngsters identify the number rods mark each rod with lines spaced ½" apart. See how rod 1 has no marks and rod 10 has 9 lines on it—one line for each ½" increment of length.

Shopping List	
Quantity	**Description**
5 feet	½" × 6" pine
4 feet	¼" × ¾" pine lattice

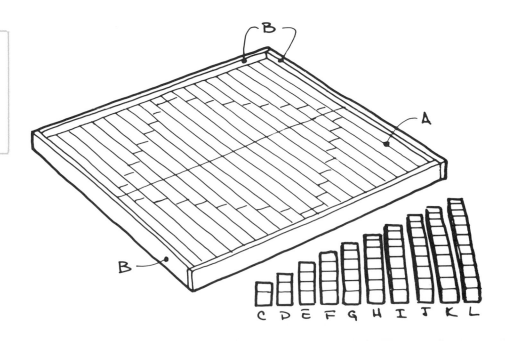

Parts List

Part	Name	No.	Size	Material
A	Base	1	½″ × 10⅛″ × 10⅛″	pine
B	Sides	4	¼″ × ¾″ × 10⅜″	pine lattice
C	Block 1	8	½″ × ½″ × ½″	pine
D	Block 2	8	½″ × ½″ × 1″	pine
E	Block 3	8	½″ × ½″ × 1½″	pine
F	Block 4	8	½″ × ½″ × 2″	pine
G	Block 5	8	½″ × ½″ × 2½″	pine
H	Block 6	8	½″ × ½″ × 3″	pine
I	Block 7	8	½″ × ½″ × 3½″	pine
J	Block 8	8	½″ × ½″ × 4″	pine
K	Block 9	8	½″ × ½″ × 4½″	pine
L	Block 10	4	½″ × ½″ × 5″	pine

146

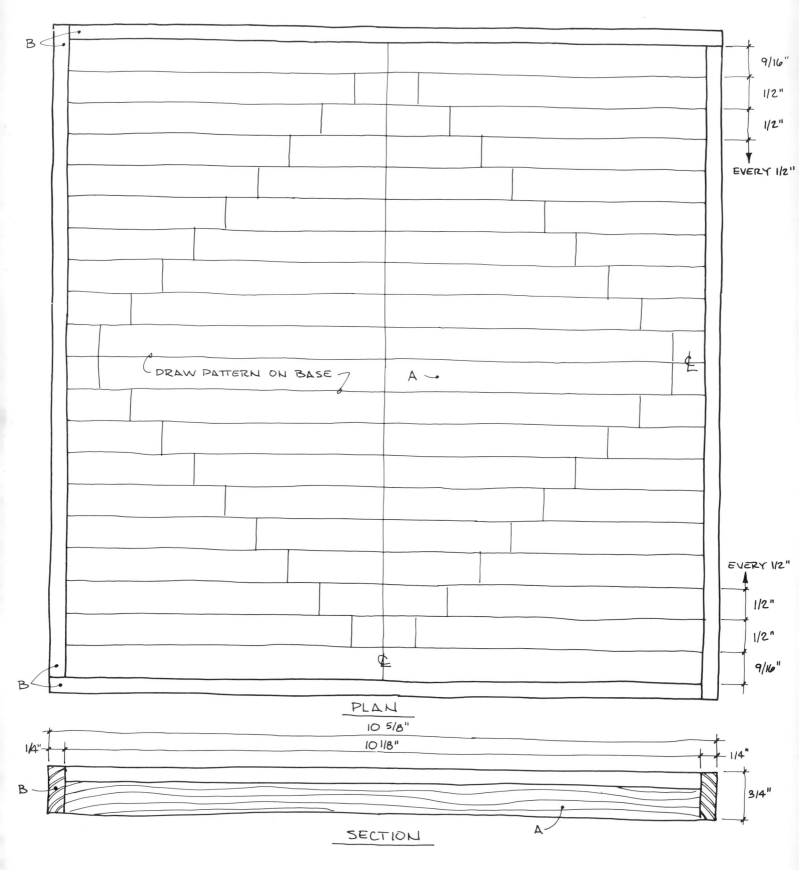

9/16"

1/2"

1/2"

EVERY 1/2"

DRAW PATTERN ON BASE

A

₵

₵

EVERY 1/2"

1/2"

1/2"

9/16"

B

B

PLAN

10 5/8"

10 1/8"

1/4"

1/4"

B

3/4"

A

SECTION

PEGGED PLAY BOARD

Learning is fun and games with this teach-yourself activity board designed to challenge and entertain toddlers. Its colorful shaped parts fit onto the pegged board and stack one on top of the other.

BEGIN CONSTRUCTION by gluing two ¾"-thick pine boards together to make a board at least 12½" wide. Lay out the base (A), which is a 12"-dia. circle on this piece of wood. Cut it to shape with a coping or saber saw.

Make patterns for cutting and drilling the play parts by enlarging the shape of parts (C–G) and transferring this to a piece of stiff cardboard or ⅛" hardboard. Mark the location and drill the ⅜" peg holes through the patterns.

Arrange the patterns on the base according to the plan. Use the patterns to locate all peg holes on the base. Drill these holes as straight as possible; slanted peg holes will cause alignment problems when they try to place the pentagons (F) and hexagons (G) over their pegs. Make these holes ½" deep using tape as a depth gauge.

Cut the pegs to length from ⅜" dowel stock. Round their tops slightly with #120 grit sandpaper, then glue them to the base.

Use the part patterns to trace the shape of the circles (B), oblongs (C), triangles (D), squares (E), pentagons (F), and hexagons (G). Cut these parts out of ½" pine stock.

After you have cut out a set of parts stack them together and sand the sides smooth. This will save time and assure that the parts in each set are the same. Enlarge the peg holes in the patterns to ½" and use these patterns as a guide when drilling the peg holes in each part.

We finished the base and pegs with a wipe-on oil and painted the play pieces in primary colors with high-gloss enamel.

Shopping List

Quantity	Description
2 feet	¾" × 8" pine
7 feet	½" × 6" pine
2	⅜" dia. × 3 foot hardwood dowel

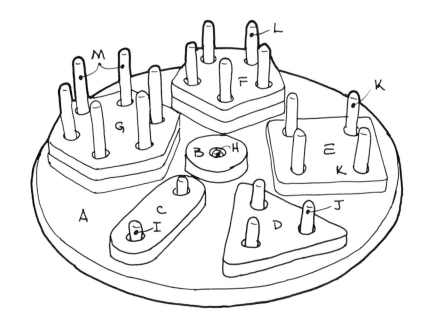

Parts List

Part	Name	No.	Size	Material
A	Base	1	¾″ × 12″ dia.	pine
B	Circle	1	cut from pattern	½″ pine
C	Oblongs	2	cut from pattern	½″ pine
D	Triangles	3	cut from pattern	½″ pine
E	Squares	4	cut from pattern	½″ pine
F	Pentagons	5	cut from pattern	½″ pine
G	Hexagons	6	cut from pattern	½″ pine
H	Circle peg	1	⅜″ dia. × 1″	hardwood dowel
I	Oblong pegs	2	⅜″ dia. × 1½″	hardwood dowel
J	Triangle pegs	3	⅜″ dia. × 2″	hardwood dowel
K	Square pegs	4	⅜″ dia. × 2½″	hardwood dowel
L	Pentagon pegs	5	⅜″ dia. × 3″	hardwood dowel
M	Hexagon pegs	6	⅜″ dia. × 3½″	hardwood dowel

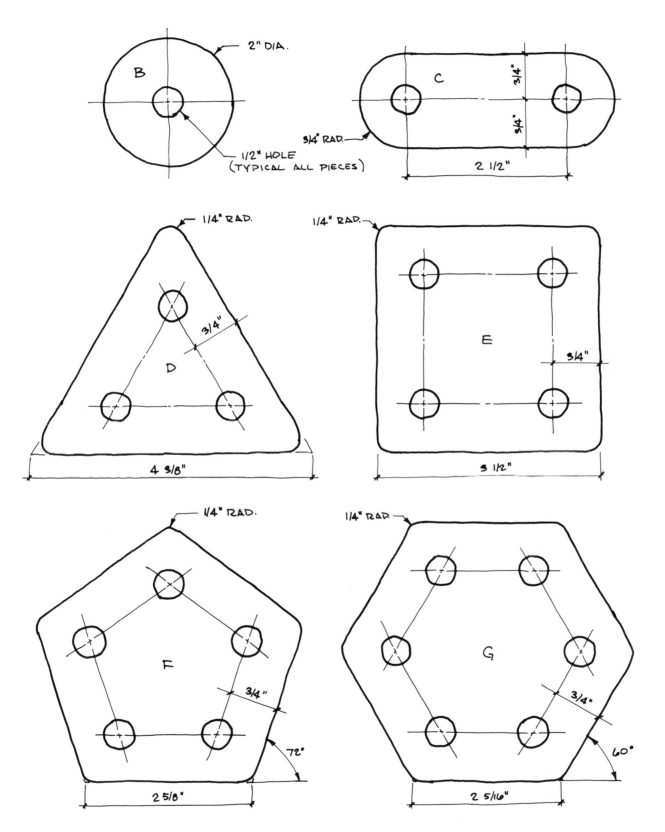

DETAILS PARTS B THRU G

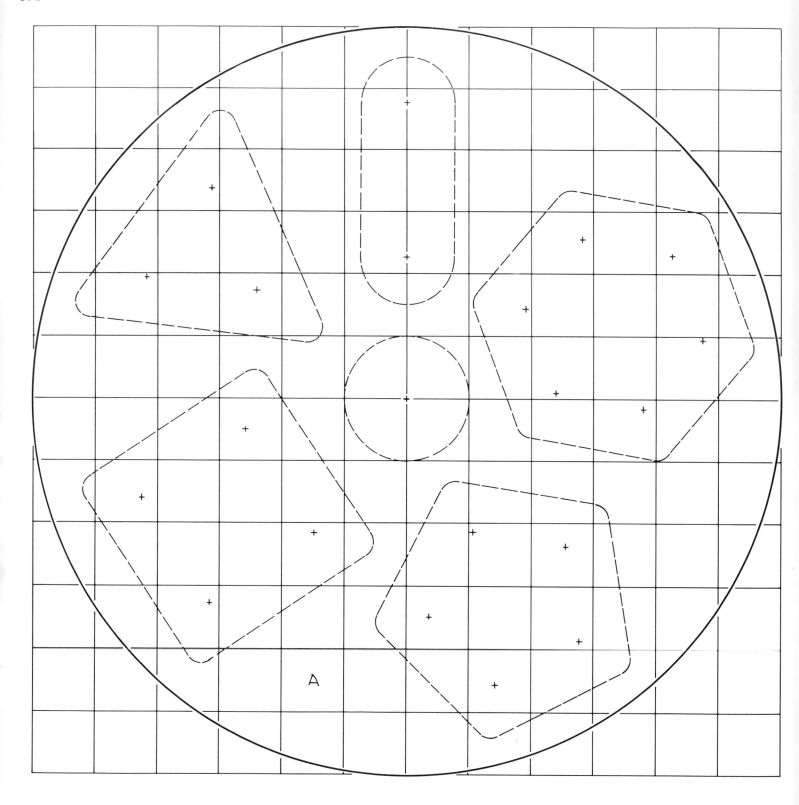

A

OTHER BOOKS FROM SEDGEWOOD® PRESS: